Ask Asha

To Chie,

May you find
wisdom & joy
in these teachings
of the Masters.
Joy,
Asha

Ask Asha

Heartfelt Answers *to* Everyday
Dilemmas *on the* Spiritual Path

Asha Praver

Crystal Clarity Publishers, Nevada City, CA 95959
Copyright © 2014 Hansa Trust
All rights reserved. Published 2014

Printed in USA

ISBN 13: 978-1-56589-290-3
ePub ISBN: 978-1-56589-553-9

Cover design and interior design and layout by Tejindra Scott Tully

---

Library of Congress Cataloging-in-Publication Data Available

---

 www.crystalclarity.com | 800.424.1055 – 530.478.7600

*Dedicated to
Swami Kriyananda*

Table of Contents

A few words from the author ...

The dilemmas raised and resolved here are from truth seekers around the world, sent to the *Ask Asha* feature of my website. Even when the answer meanders through many aspects of the spiritual path, all have a practical immediacy not always present in mere theoretical discussions.

Perhaps you've never faced these exact situations: Giving up a child for adoption, trying to forgive a philandering spouse, facing the death of a beloved pet—to name a few included here.

Still, all of us have suffered guilt, disappointment, heartbreak, and anxiety about the state of the world. The details may differ from what you face, but the solutions will still prove to be of value.

My own spiritual training has come over four decades of life in the Ananda communities guided by Swami Kriyananda, a disciple of the Indian guru, Paramhansa Yogananda.

Yogananda's *Autobiography of a Yogi* is a textbook for those seeking a spiritual rather than merely a religious life. *Religion* too often is about dogma and form. *Spirituality* is the consciousness with which we live. The cutting edge of learning is when high ideals are tested in the cold light of day.

The Ananda communities are not remote monasteries sheltering a world-renouncing few, but active centers of work and service, home to people in all stages of life. Marriage, children, money, education, creative work—all aspects of life must be faced and resolved in a spiritual way.

May the solutions offered—and the deep learning that inspired them—be for you, as they have been for me, the doorway to happiness.

Asha Praver
www.NayaswamiAsha.org

In this book, Swami Kriyananda is called *Swamiji*

Paramhansa Yogananda is called *Master*

*Special thanks to Jack Wallace
for invaluable help in editing this book*

Ask Asha

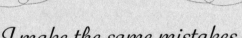

I make the same mistakes over and over.

Despite my best intentions, I can't seem to make any spiritual progress. Everyday life also confuses me. If, as the scriptures say, this world is a dream, why work so hard to succeed? Compared to divine realization, isn't everything else trivial?

EVERY APPLE SEED contains within it the potential to become a fruit-bearing tree. It doesn't happen all at once though. It may be tiresome for the seed first to sprout, then be a twig, then a sapling; but it is the fastest, in fact the *only* way to become a tree. There are inescapable stages of development.

So it is with the soul. Self-realization is our divine destiny, but we can't get there in one leap. Perhaps your repeated failure is not caused by lack of will power but lack of patience—trying to reach the goal without first walking the path.

It is tempting to say, for example, if renunciation is required, "Now I must renounce! If austerities are beneficial, let me banish all comfort from my life!" You may think this proof of your dedication, but in fact it is looking for a shortcut that isn't there.

If you reach too far beyond your actual realization, inevitably you will collapse back, perhaps to a place lower than where you started. You may think you are compromising your ideals to aim for less, but for you this may be the surest route to success.

Spiritual progress is both science and art. The science is comprised of the divine laws of the universe; the art is knowing which to apply and when.

About everyday life, I used to share your confusion. If everything in this world is ephemeral, why bother? Intuitively I felt compelled to strive for excellence, but philosophically I couldn't figure out why. In Swamiji's book, *The Essence of the Bhagavad Gita*, I found the answer.

He speaks of the Self-realized person as *triguna rahitam*. This means one who has transcended the three *gunas*—the fluctuating energies that make up the material world. *Tamo guna* is confining, darkening, downward pulling. *Rajo guna* is activating, restless. *Sattwa guna* is uplifting and calm.

To determine what is forward for you spiritually, ask yourself, "What guna, or combination of gunas, am I expressing?" Eventually we must go beyond the material world altogether, leaving even sattwa guna behind, but like the seed becoming a tree, we have to get there in stages.

"Why bother? Nothing is real." This may *sound* like philosophical truth, but it is more likely tamo guna—fear and laziness *masquerading* as wisdom. Superficially, lazy resembles calm, but they are at opposite ends of the spectrum. Fear is paralyzing. Better to be intensely active, even restless in your activity, than succumb to either. The first victory must be over tamo guna.

Imagine the rim of a bicycle wheel with spokes leading into the center. We are all spread out at different points around the rim. The way to reach the center depends on how the rim is oriented from your point of view.

Those at the bottom must go up; those at the top, down. For some, more discipline is required; others need to relax and go with the flow. If the opposites happen to meet, each may declare, "Only my way is right!" They don't see that *progress is directional, in relation to the center.*

If Mahatma Gandhi, in the middle of the movement to free India, had decided to use his fame instead to open a law practice, everyone would say he had fallen. If a lazy, do-nothing man finally got off the couch, went to law school, and made a fortune, everyone would say, "Well done!"

Imagine now that the points on the rim are aspects of your own karma. Eventually all karma must be resolved in God, but you can't do it in one swoop. You have to move step-by-step, according to where you are in relation to the center.

On the path of Self-realization there is no manual of *Right Behavior* you can put on like a uniform. You expand from within—like a seed—from the heart of your being. Dogmas won't do it; intuition is needed.

When Jesus was asked, "How can you tell a true prophet from a false one?" he answered, "By their fruits ye shall know them." The answer to "Why bother?" is the same: "Look at the fruits."

Think of that man lying on the couch, letting others support him. No matter how highfalutin' his philosophy, he is a lazy bum.

This world is a spiritual gymnasium. The equipment is the circumstances your karma has brought. Even if you go to the gym every day, though, just sitting there won't make you strong. You have to run the treadmill and lift the weights.

What you accomplish in life may be unimportant compared to eternity, but the *consciousness* you develop in order to succeed is the path to freedom.

Great masters and highly-evolved souls know far better than we do the dream nature of this world. Still, they set the example by working hard to accomplish what God has given them to do.

Swamiji would go over a manuscript dozens of times before he considered it ready for publication. Even after a book was printed, he would edit it again, if he felt it could be improved.

When members of our community were first learning to sing his music, Swamiji would often stop them mid-performance to correct something. Certain people objected. Correcting singers in public was embarrassing, they said.

"They need to put out the energy to do it right," Swamiji replied.

Singing wrong notes was only a symptom. Laziness and lack of concentration—tamo guna—was the more important problem to be overcome. Learning to sing properly was a way of training their consciousness. Most knew this, and welcomed Swamiji's guidance.

As my mother aged, her body began to fail. Everyday tasks became more and more of a challenge. "Getting old is not for sissies!" she often said. The same is true of the path. The first essential attitude for the devotee is courage.

In my mother's struggle with her body, defeat was inevitable. No physical body lasts forever. Nor does every seed become a tree. By contrast, on the spiritual path, victory is assured. It is not a matter of *if*, but *when*.

To my everlasting embarrassment, I remember a conversation I had with Swamiji once when tamo guna had me in its grip. Actually, it wasn't a conversation, because Swamiji said nothing.

I was facing a big challenge. To be fair, it was a serious, lifelong issue, and I was far from the finish line.

"Everything in my life is going well, except this one thing. I would be so happy if it would just go away!"

In other words: *If the spiritual path were not so hard, it would be easier.*

Silent and expressionless, Swamiji stared at me, my words hanging in the air between us, as tears of self-pity rolled down my cheeks.

Several moments passed. Then the phone rang. Swamiji answered it without even a glance of apology. It was to confirm a doctor's appointment he had been trying to arrange. When the call ended, so did the interview.

Don't think for a moment that Swamiji was being rude. Even then I knew his response was brilliant: *Stop whining!*

I shudder to think what might have happened if he had shown even an ounce of sympathy. I would have clung to it like a drowning person to a log. It would not, however, have been my raft over the ocean of delusion, but a stone taking me to the bottom of the sea.

I persevered. What choice did I have? Either wallow in misery, or make an effort to transcend it. I can't say even now that I have *conquered* that delusion, but by the grace of God it no longer defines me.

The pathway to success is paved with failure. There is no alternate route.

To rail against yourself for repeated failure gives tamo guna the win, eroding your confidence and sapping your strength. It doesn't matter if you have been over the same ground a thousand times. If it is where you find yourself, the only thing to do is move forward from there. ⮑

Nothing outside ordinary reality ever happens to me.

My friends have all kinds of spiritual experiences. But for three years I've meditated twice a day, every day; yet I've not heard AUM, nor seen the spiritual eye. No voices, lights, visible auras, vibrating crystals, or miracles of any kind. My life is blessed with love, inspiration, and inspiring dreams. Desires are slipping away or fulfilled in surprising ways. But I am going one hundred percent on belief, and find it hard to develop devotion. Sometimes I feel equivocal even about the good things that have happened. A little experience would tip the balance from belief to faith. Already I am middle-aged. How long must I wait?

S O MANY WONDERFUL THINGS are happening, and still you wonder. Doubt is a special kind of purgatory, taking the sunlight out of the brightest day.

In his autobiography, *The New Path*, Swamiji writes of his own struggle with doubt. The solution he discovered is love. Alas, you are doubly stymied—because you doubt, you are unwilling to love.

I don't know if anything I say can break the cycle, but let me try. Allow me to rewrite your letter as a note from your son to you:

> *Dear Dad,*
>
> *Thanks so much for bringing me up. We've got a great home. I love my room. The meals are terrific, and when I raid the refrigerator, something good is always there. My clothes are awesome. I love my bike. You picked the best school, and even help with homework.*
>
> *Still, two of my friends have motorcycles. Why can't I get one? How many times have I told you about this? You say you love me, but I'm fourteen already! How much longer do I have to wait?*
>
> *Your son*

You are God's child for eternity. His love is unconditional, omnipresent. Your very existence is proof of His everlasting commitment.

And how have you—*we*—responded? For more incarnations than we can imagine, we have turned our backs on the only One who truly loves us. Madly we have pursued every possible dead end, looking for love in all the wrong places. Finally it has occurred to us that maybe, just *maybe*, God is the answer.

I heard an interview on the radio with two men in their early twenties who became gazillionaires when a company they dropped out of college to form went public.

"You have earned a hundred times more money than your fathers did in a lifetime," the interviewer said. "How do you feel about that?"

The gazillionaires, surprised he would ask, said emphatically, "We gave *two years of our lives* to build this company!"

God has been faithful to us; it is *we* who have strayed. We are in no position to demand tokens of His commitment. Yet you have been showered with them. Ah, but there is more on your list! Like a child at Christmas, you compare your letter to Santa with the presents under the tree and feel shortchanged.

Being a devotee is not a business transaction. It is a relationship of selfless love.

Are you persuaded when your son says, "If you loved me, you'd buy me a motorcycle?" More gifts equal more love: Is that the example you want to set for him? Is that the example God wants to set for you?

There is no standard of proof that God must meet. So far you have been willing to put your mind behind your beliefs, but not yet risk your heart. If you withhold your love from God, who will suffer? God or you?

When Swamiji was living with Master at Mt. Washington, a monk there had many experiences of the kind you hope to receive. Swamiji had none. In the end, that monk left the spiritual path. Those experiences were not a sign of favor, but Master's effort to save him from delusion.

Nothing outside ordinary reality ever happens to me.

Perhaps what God wants from you is the courage to open your heart without the final proof you seek. "My ways are not thy ways, saith the Lord." There comes a point in every relationship, human or divine, when you have to go with your heart.

You are holding on to a dangerously mistaken notion that because your friends have certain experiences, they are more advanced, or more favored by God. Comparing yourself to others won't help you develop devotion, nor will it create the magnetism to draw God's love.

If you give your son that motorcycle, will it secure his love or will he demand further proof? When he's sixteen, a car? If God gives you lights, will you next need a miracle, then another, to prove the first wasn't merely coincidence?

Once you start down the road of weighing and measuring love, there is no end to it. No relationship can thrive in such an atmosphere. You have to love God because it is your nature to love Him, and God's nature to love you.

From your perspective, it is impossible to know in which direction freedom lies. Like you with your son, God knows the road ahead better than you. Don't pray for lights and sounds— seek devotion *with* devotion. Accept with gratitude all that He has given, and in return, give Him your heart. ❧

Spiritual hypocrisy has left a bad taste in my mouth.

In the church where I grew up, public displays of piety were the norm, usually by ignorant, even mean-spirited people. True divine feelings, I decided, should be kept within the heart. I have a deep inner life now, and many spiritual friends; but group activities, especially public worship, are hard for me. I participate only because my Guru says it is important. I used to think my reluctance was a virtue. Now I think it is a hang-up. Can you help?

*F*REEDOM IS THE GOAL of the spiritual path, freedom from all limiting ideas and self-definitions. *Moksha* is the Sanskrit word. Stages toward *moksha* include freeing one-self from subconscious habits, unexamined ideas, and compulsions based on false premises. Your aversion to public worship fits nicely into the category of things to be overcome.

Reason follows feeling, Master often said. If you are predisposed toward a point of view, you will find endless ways to justify it. It is quite common for the aspiring devotee to use true spiritual principles to reach false conclusions.

Fortunately, you have noticed!

Each devotee has his or her own relationship with God. *Bhav* is the Sanskrit word, meaning "spiritual attitude" or way of approaching the Divine. Some people are by nature deeply private, others more outwardly expressive. It isn't a matter of right or wrong.

Certain principles, however, apply to all. The important one here is *magnetism*. Master said that whether your energy flows outward to the world or inward toward God depends to a large extent on the company you keep. *Environment is stronger than will power.*

Unless you live in complete solitude—and even then, subtle vibrations still affect you—you are always in some kind of magnetic field generated by the consciousness of those around you. Even alone in your own home, you have neighbors whose thoughts and feelings bombard you constantly.

The deeper your inner life, and therefore the stronger your own magnetism, the less you will be affected. But it is naïve to imagine you are not affected at all.

During the years he was earning money to start Ananda, Swamiji lived in San Francisco. His apartment was in a quiet area, well off the street, and in terms of noise, exactly the same day or night. Still, it *felt* quieter at night, and more conducive to meditation and creative thinking. Everyone around was asleep, freeing the atmosphere of their restless thoughts.

Environmental influence is cumulative and lingering. When you cut onions, days later you may still get a whiff from your hands. Simply having been near onions may cause your clothes to reek.

Thought vibrations are more powerful than mere onions. It is wise to immerse yourself, whenever possible, in that which you seek to make your own. This is why Master spoke so forcefully about the importance of spiritual communities. Jesus, too, encouraged his disciples to live together.

This is *satsang*, meaning "the company of truth." Yes, hanging out with high-minded people is satsang; but when we chant and pray, meditate or listen to a discourse together, the focused magnetism is more powerful than just having a meal.

In an interview Swamiji gave about the importance of the Festival of Light—the ritual we do at Ananda on Sundays—he said that even when people meditate in the same room together, often they do not meditate *together*, in the sense of uniting their energy to help one another spiritually.

Whenever he meditated with others, Swamiji said he consciously meditated *with* and *for* them. Why not think of public worship like that? Let it be a time of *giving* to others. Pray on their behalf. Chant whole-heartedly. The depth of your devotion will help others, also, to go deep.

In the early years of Ananda, when we all lived together at the Village, there was no question of not going to Sunday Service. Participating with energy was an act of friendship. The mere repetition of the minister's words did not in itself create the experience. What made it powerful was the commitment by each of us to go deep into Spirit, together.

"When enough people call sincerely enough," Swamiji writes, "a mighty flow from the river of grace is deflected toward this planet; a new ray of Light is drawn downward, and all who tune in to it are uplifted as they never could be, were they to struggle merely on their own."

Imagine if you were living in some remote area, the only devotee for miles around. How you would *hunger* for the opportunity to share your inspiration with others! You have the good karma to be in good company. Embrace it with gratitude. ⤴

My job and the rewards
it offers seem pointless.

All I want is a simple life of yoga and meditation.
As a result, my performance at work is taking a beating.
Recently I was caught in an unhealthy relationship,
but went through it completely consciously.
Now that I fully understand the workings of ego in
human relationships, I no longer want to participate.
I only want to find and experience truth.
Day and night, all I can think of is God.

*A*FTER A LONG STRUGGLE, it is tempting to claim total victory. Better, though, to be humble about your understanding. Otherwise, you may miss important lessons that come later.

"Now that I'm spiritual, I want to leave everything behind." Would that it were so simple! Rarely is this a good idea at the early stage people often propose it. The roots of karma run deep. Simplify, yes. Do yoga and meditation. Renounce as much as you can. In spiritual matters there is no point in being timid. Still, Master cautions, "Be practical in your idealism."

If a dramatic gesture lacks the proper foundation, it will not bring the results you seek. It can work against you, in fact, causing you to seesaw between extremes rather than making steady, spiritual progress.

What would you do if you left your job? Where would you go? Great saints can leave home with no more security than the continuously repeated name of God. But such souls are rare. Recently you have contemplated marriage and children. Now you want renunciation. Perhaps you should give your spiritual ardor time to ripen.

God has so arranged this world that we have to live with others and work for a living. Annoying as that can be, it is no accident. Our spirituality is tested in the cold light of day. Job and home are the proving ground.

The skills required for success in the world are the same needed to find God: courage, calmness, concentration—and creativity—to name just a few.

If you renounce prematurely, instead of soaring in God, you may actually fall. With no responsibilities or fixed schedule, laziness too often creeps in, and you end up spending *less* time on spiritual pursuits.

At this stage in your life, rather than leaving your job, it would be better to bring God into your work. Apply yourself, but from a higher perspective. In every interaction, ask God to guide you, to make you His instrument. "Lord, how can I serve You in this person or task?"

If your work is creative, ask God to give you good ideas. If mundane, ask Him to entertain you with His bliss. Silently chant, or repeat a name of God dear to you. Use your time at work exactly as you would if you weren't on the job: thinking of God. If that is difficult, consider it a challenge He has given you, and one that He will help you overcome.

Even Lahiri Mahasaya—after initiation by Babaji and awakening to his destiny as the founder of the Kriya Yoga line—continued to work for many years as an accountant, serving his family and community in seemingly mundane ways. Nothing in itself is unspiritual. It only seems so when we fail to bring to it the right understanding.

Live the simple life of yoga and meditation you long for, even if much of the day is taken up otherwise. If you renounce prematurely, the karma will merely return, likely in more difficult form. Embrace what God has given you, and your very sincerity will attract new opportunities. Then, with a free heart, you can move on. ❧

My partner cheated on me for fifteen years.

Finally I separated from him, but now he wants me back. He explains away what happened as being caused by the pain of an undiagnosed mental condition. He says he is healed now and wants to grow spiritually with me. Can people change? Does love forgive everything, including infidelity?

*Y*OU WOULD BE WISE to purge from your heart whatever anger you may still have towards this man. To see yourself as a victim, to feel the world *owes* you a certain standard of behavior, is to doom yourself to disappointment. The most important reason to forgive him—even for infidelity—is for your own peace of mind.

Don't whitewash what he did, though, in an attempt to overcome your negativity. To hide from the truth is not the same as forgiveness. True forgiveness comes when you face squarely the reality of what happened, and then see it from a higher perspective. We all make mistakes. Sometimes, egregious ones. Divine Mother understands, and forgives our transgressions. It behooves us to see one another through Her eyes.

As to whether you take him back, that is an entirely different question. Divine Mother also enforces quite impersonally the appropriate consequences for our wrong actions. In this, too, we must emulate Her.

Everyone can change, of course. Our state of consciousness is not fixed. As Master says, "A saint is a sinner who never gave up." In essence, we are all equally children of God. Some manifest that divinity clearly; others hide behind clouds of egoic, self-interest.

Just because a person declares himself healed does not make him so. Only time will tell. One thing you say does make me wonder. *He* explains away *what happened as caused by the pain he was suffering.*

True healing includes taking responsibility and, as much as possible, making amends. In the Twelve Step Program, for example, you face those you hurt, and fix what you broke. That's not always possible, but you have to try.

To *explain* is not the same as taking responsibility. Even more concerning is to explain *away*, as you have put it. Self-justification is not healing.

A man lived at Ananda for a dozen years, entirely on his own terms. We allow for a great deal of eccentricity, but his complete unwillingness to contribute as others did eventually led to a parting of the ways.

He never accepted responsibility for what happened. Later, claiming to have "inside information" from his years at Ananda, he did his best to discredit the community, Swamiji, and many of his former friends. His malicious lies caused great harm.

Years later, with the dust long settled, I happened to see him again. He came on with great friendliness, talking to me about the importance of forgiveness. It was my spiritual duty, he said, to heal the breach between us, and take him back as a friend.

"Have you changed?" I asked. "Do you repudiate your past? Will you apologize, and make amends for the damage you've done?"

His answer was carefully crafted. "I'm sorry some of you suffered."

"That's no answer. Are you sorry for the part you played in causing that suffering?"

He said nothing, but his silence spoke volumes.

Rather than accept responsibility for his own wrong actions, he tried to convince me that *I* would be wrong not to welcome him back with open arms.

He is a child of God, yes. Surely he *could* change; but clearly, he had not.

I bear him no ill will. His wrong actions are between him and Divine Mother. But I do have to respond appropriately.

"It would be irresponsible of me to welcome you back," I said. "You haven't repudiated any of the attitudes that caused so much harm. Why would I invite you to make trouble all over again?"

As to your ex-partner, certainly he can change. But where is the proof? Be practical. Is his mental suffering over? Has he developed the strength of character not to pass his pain on to others? Naturally you hope so, but don't let hope blind you.

Take your time. If his transformation is real, he will understand he has to *win* your trust. And if he doesn't, that itself is sign enough. ❧

People will take advantage if we forgive everything.

They'll do whatever they feel like doing, then say they've changed, and all will be forgiven. How will that help anyone?

ORGIVENESS is a complicated subject. Each person has karma to work out. Simple, happy endings are rare.

On one side is the person who feels hurt. On the other side is the one who seemingly caused the injury. Then there is how you feel in your heart, compared with how you respond outwardly. Each has to be considered separately.

From the beginning of my spiritual life, I adopted a policy Swamiji suggested: Try to understand every question from the highest perspective. For me, this means asking: How would Master respond? What would Swamiji do?

You would expect the lives of saints to be free of disharmony. The opposite is true. Great souls seem to attract betrayal, usually from those to whom they have opened their hearts. There are many reasons for this. One is the dual nature of the universe. Whenever light ascends, darkness tries to snuff it out. Not a pleasant thought, but proven true, time and again.

People like us incarnate because our karma compels us. We have many unlearned lessons to face. Masters come only to set an example of how to live in this world. They have no karma of their own. They take on the appearance of karma, or the karma of their disciples, to show us how to behave.

Several of Master's longtime disciples later turned against him, even dragging him into court, trying to destroy his work and reputation. After one treacherous person left the ashram and moved to another part of the country, every year, Master sent him a case of mangoes. Every year, the box was returned unopened.

Master said it would be several more lifetimes before that disciple reconciled with his Guru. After that, however, he would quickly achieve liberation. Though he appeared to be far less advanced than disciples who never strayed, Master knew he was more advanced than most. He just had a little bit of karma to work out—a few more lifetimes—then he would be free forever.

This, for one reason, is why we should not judge. Though a person may not be showing proper restraint, the totality of his spiritual and karmic condition must also be taken into account. There is no simple formula.

Swamiji had to endure extraordinary persecution from his fellow disciples. In an effort to destroy both his reputation and life's work, they filed a massive lawsuit against him that dragged on for over a decade, and pushed Ananda to the brink of bankruptcy. His persecutors then tried to seize the copyrights to Swamiji's books and music, not to publish but to bury them.

Swamiji fought back. It was not *dharma* to give up his work for Master merely because others opposed it. But he never let the battle affect him personally. His love for his brothers and sisters was unchanged. It was to their souls, not their outward behavior, that he gave his loyalty.

Consider the crucifixion of Jesus, and his immortal words, "Father, forgive them, for they know not what they do." This level of forgiveness may be beyond us now, but it is where we are heading, and one day will arrive.

When I face a difficult situation, I try to keep in mind this thought: *God knows what He is doing.* I may have an opinion, but *He knows.* Even if the situation seems completely unfair, *God knows what He is doing.* He can be trusted to bring me what I need at the time I need it. And to give me the strength to use what He sends for my own highest good.

Even if I can't get there right away and have to endure long days and nights of wrong thinking before right attitude comes, I do my best not to define myself by my mistakes.

I make a distinction between those actions I *commit* and those to which I am *committed.* Even in the worst of times, a part of me remembers: Error is temporary. Goodness is eternal. I *will* get over it.

All we ever experience is our own consciousness. When we cling to wrong attitudes, we feel miserable. Even if circumstances justify our suffering, the real question is: *Who suffers?*

I read a touching article about a woman whose daughter was murdered. Even after the murderer was sent to prison for life, the mother continued to seethe. Finally she realized that anger was killing her. The man who took the life of her child was taking hers as well. She decided to go to the prison and confront him in the hope of finding some resolution.

At first it was hard to be in the same room. Still, she had no choice but to persevere. Gradually she began to see him not as a monster, but as a fellow human being who had also suffered. In the end, she became like a mother to him.

She didn't condone what he had done, but she accepted it as a reality that had to be faced. Expansion of consciousness happened also for him. Only by getting to know the bereaved mother did he understand the suffering he had caused.

When the murderer truly repented, the mother was able to open her heart to him. She became a channel of the all-forgiving love of God. "The channel is blessed by that which flows through it," Master says. She was healed.

All of us are on a journey toward Self-realization. Any progress along the way should be celebrated. If a friend has repented of wrong behavior, then it is not lowering one's standards to welcome him back with open arms. To do so is to affirm the potential in all of us.

If a person proves incapable of responding in a noble way to the love you give him—that is cause for compassion, not a reason for resentment. But to let that person believe wrong actions have no consequences is not forgiveness. Usually it is fear or guilt trying to pass itself off as something more elevated.

A friend of mine has had a difficult time with an elderly relative. The relative has done everything possible to take the joy out of her life. She was recounting something he said, when I interrupted.

"You let him talk to you like that?"

"I did."

"I would have asked him to stop. If he refused, I would have walked out. You don't have to leave angry, but you can still leave! You're not doing him a favor letting him treat you like that."

Now if my friend had not been affected by his unkind words, I would have responded differently. Giving love to an unhappy old man would be a valuable service.

She had, however, been deeply affected.

All of us are *equal* before God. Everyone's karma has to be considered. You are not more important than others, but neither are they more important than you.

Humility is not self-abnegation. It is self-honesty—seeing things as they are. It is a question of *dharma*, of doing what is right.

Years ago a woman wrote to Swamiji, saying that she was leaving her husband after seven years of marriage. "When I meditate, he turns on the TV as loud as possible. He mocks me when I speak of spiritual things."

"She put up with that for *seven years*?" Swamiji said. "I wouldn't have taken it for fifteen minutes!"

When I was new on the path, I became angry with a friend I felt had mistreated me. Over several months, I found my inner diatribe focused on a few, specific incidents. *Why only these?*

I came to understand that, in those situations, true principles had been at stake. I had known that at the time, but hadn't had the courage to speak up.

My friend, by contrast, had not been aware. He had done the best he could, with the understanding he had. To be angry with him was like railing at a three-year-old for not knowing how to read. So I got angry with myself instead! It was better than blaming him, though not by much.

Finally I was able to see myself the way I saw him: *I had done the best I could with the understanding I had.* What more can we ask of ourselves or each other? His error was in not understanding dharma; mine was not having the courage to act on what I knew to be true.

I am not proud of my cowardice, but neither am I ashamed. Ignorance is a necessary stage on the path to wisdom.

The most important thing is not how forgiveness affects others, but how *not* forgiving affects you. There is a certain perverse pleasure in holding on to a grudge, but letting it go brings far greater joy. Try it and see. ༄

I loved a powerful and good man, but he died.

My love for him and my attachment to being a "one-man woman" keeps me from giving my heart to anyone else, though I long to have a close relationship now.

*L*OYALTY IS THE FIRST LAW of God," Master says. In order to accomplish anything in life, we have to commit ourselves, and persevere in our commitment. Nothing great is ever achieved without will power.

It is essential, though, to be loyal to the right thing—to *principles*—to truth itself—not merely to the *form* those principles take.

A spiritual organization, for example, may sometimes give primary loyalty to itself, not to the ideals on which it was founded. It may even condone dishonorable behavior in the name of self-preservation. This is a grave mistake. When loyalty shifts from principle to form, it easily becomes callous, fanatical, or foolish.

Some spiritual traditions assert that divorce is a sin. Fickleness is no virtue, but neither is it always right for a couple to stay together, especially at the expense of either partner's spiritual potential. Some lifelong couples inspire. Others look merely worn out.

I recall a woman widowed after sixty years of marriage. A devotee tried to comfort her by saying, "You'll see your husband again," meaning in heaven.

"Sixty years was long enough!" she replied.

Compared to eternity, one incarnation is an insignificant period of time. Consciousness expands from life to life in a continuous process. Death changes nothing except the context in which we seek realization.

The *form* of the man you loved is gone forever. The *essence* of what you love in each other, though, is untouched, even by death.

In the astral world, we meet those we have been close to in the incarnation just finished, as well as many other lifetimes. There is no jealousy. No thought that loving one means others cannot be loved. While physical form imposes limitation, love itself knows no boundary.

Sometimes a relationship is given to us, then taken away, and we know we've had the love of our life and there won't be another. In our grief, there comes also the certainty that what God has given, and what He has taken away, are spiritually correct.

When Master's mother died, he and several of his siblings were quite young. His father never married again, but took on the task of being both father and mother to his eight children. Years later, Master tried to engage a female servant to take care of him. Adamantly, his father refused.

"Service to me ended with your mother. I will not accept ministrations from any other woman."

Always a deeply spiritual man, after his wife's passing he lived an exemplary life of austerity and devotion to God.

I don't think your experience is the same as Master's father. Your attachment to being a "one-woman man" seems more a romantic notion than a sincere expression of your actual state of consciousness.

Maybe you'll have another deep relationship in this lifetime, maybe not. Karma determines everything. It is not, however, more noble "never to love again." Why would loving one person make it wrong to love another in the same or an even greater way?

Give your loyalty to Love itself.

A friend came to me when his wife was pregnant with their second child. Eyes full of tears, he said, "How can I be a good father to this baby? I love my first-born so much. I can't imagine loving anyone else like that."

All I could say was "Love is infinite. Don't worry." Soon after the child was born, he saw me again.

"You were right."

Be completely sincere with God. Tell Him of your longings, and also your confusion. Pour it into Divine Mother's lap. Follow Master's advice for how to pray: "Be convinced that God has heard you, then go on about your duties, seeking not to know if He will grant your request."

Talk to Him whenever your heart feels restless. If it is beneficial, God will send you a partner. If not, know that God is helping you grow in other ways. While that may not be easy to accept, the way to get through karma is to learn what it has to teach, facing it with courage, calmness, and joy. ❧

The husband my parents have chosen for me is not my soul-mate.

They think the marriage is perfect, and will bring me great happiness. He's a good person, but I'm not attracted to him. All I have ever asked of God is that my husband be my soul-mate. I feel bitter towards both my parents and God.

I AM CONCERNED FOR YOU, and even more for your husband-to-be. To enter a marriage unwillingly is a recipe for disaster. Your likely response to every disappointment will be to remind your husband you never wanted to marry him in the first place. Out of consideration for his happiness, quite apart from your own, unless you can change your attitude, you should stop this marriage now.

You say you have to go along with it, but if you are old enough to get married, presumably you are old enough to get a job, a passport, and anything else you might need to live life on your own.

What you are really saying is that to refuse this marriage would be to stand up to people you are not used to defying, turning your world topsy-turvy. Not marrying him, in other words, would be highly *inconvenient*. You do, however, have a choice.

Soul-mates are a reality, but on a level far beyond romance. Master referred to it only once in all his years of teaching. He knew few could understand.

Union with your soul-mate, Master explained, comes with final liberation—*moksha*—which means transcending the physical plane. Most people consider soul-mates to be a gender-based attraction (both romantic and sexual) when, in fact, passion and desire are the greatest *obstacles* to this divine union.

Swamiji, too, was mostly silent on this until the very end of his life. The last book he wrote, *Love Perfected, Life Divine* (finished just weeks before his passing) is all about soul-mates. Beautifully written, deeply inspiring, it explains their true nature, including the self-mastery needed before such a perfect union is possible.

When you prayed to God for a soul-mate, you probably were not thinking about *moksha*. More likely, by "soul-mate," you meant someone with whom you could have a deep connection, extending also to the spiritual realm. There's nothing wrong with praying for that; but whether it is possible depends, not just on God, but also on you.

To have such a husband, you have to be that kind of wife.

Over the course of incarnations we have innumerable husbands and wives. Relationships naturally repeat; a single lifetime isn't enough to learn everything, even from one person. And life must be experienced with many souls to overcome the vast array of karmas we've accrued.

In America, we are accustomed to choosing our own partners. I wish I could tell you that the sentiment often voiced at weddings—"I have found my soul-mate!"—insures a happy marriage. Alas, it does not. So much emphasis on the unique nature of their connection can make the marriage too ego-based to survive the tests of time.

This is hard to understand, I know. I would not have understood it either when I was your age. Experience has been my teacher. Over the last decades I have presided at many weddings, and have counseled couples not just through marriage but also divorce. I've been married for over thirty years myself.

Finding your marriage partner attractive is a big plus. But the kind of instant attractiveness (especially sexual) that is so highly prized these days, is not the most important factor in success. Romantic feelings manifest for a variety of reasons, not all of them spiritually inspired, or helpful over the long haul.

The husband my parents have chosen for me is not my soul-mate.

I'm not making light of your intuition. We recognize our friends from past lives. Love at first sight does happen. What I have learned is this: It is not difficult to love. If you have a generous heart, loving is easy. The challenge is to make a life together. To build a home, raise children, earn a living, and support one another through good times and bad—that's what is hard.

This is what parents think about. Having lived long enough to raise you, they know what really counts in a marriage. In a culture where parents are involved in the choice, they look usually for lasting values, and will not be particularly interested in your ideas of attraction.

What holds a marriage together is appreciation, respect, and depth of character, which may take time to be revealed.

What kind of parents do you have? Are they insightful where you are concerned? Is their marriage inspiring? Have they earned your trust? Do they have any motive for arranging this marriage besides your happiness?

There may be social obstacles to delaying the marriage, but that could be one solution. Get to know the man and his family. Be sincere as you explore the friendship. You may still conclude this man is not your husband. Your parents are more likely to take your objection seriously if you give credence to their good intentions, even if you disagree with their judgment.

If postponement is not possible, and if, despite your hesitation, you do marry him, give the marriage your all. Be a friend to your husband. Be supportive and kind. Above all, accept responsibility. Don't blame your parents, God, or anyone else. You may be pleasantly surprised to find that, far from disappointing you, God has given you everything you hoped for in a partner.

Even if the marriage lacks the spark you hoped it would have, give your husband the sort of friendship you dreamed of sharing with the one you marry. That may awaken those same qualities in him. But if it doesn't, and your marriage proves the disappointment you fear, what will it serve you to become bitter? You may succeed in making life unpleasant for those around you, but that will pale when compared to the misery you create for yourself.

If, rather, you respond with grace to whatever God gives, your own consciousness will expand. You may then discover a wellspring of happiness within. A graceful response will also create good karma, and the magnetism to attract in some future incarnation the kind of husband you pray for now.

Small comfort, I know. I wish I could offer something better. But your present situation is the result of your past attitudes and actions. To change your destiny, change yourself. ❧

I am in love with a man who doesn't love me.

He is my colleague at work, and we used to be great friends, but not anymore. He has a new crowd and looks happy, whereas I feel very sad. I've tried to get over him, but nothing works. I can't pray for anything except to have him as my life companion.

I WOULD LIKE TO SAY: "Pray hard. Whatever you wish for will come." But I cannot do that.

Very often what we *want* is not what we *need*. No matter how strongly we pray, God will not grant our request. You have not been singled out by a cruel fate. Unrequited love is a hard lesson that many have to experience.

When the mother of a friend died a few years ago at the age of ninety, my friend sorted out her belongings. She was removing photos from their frames to put into an album. Behind a picture of her father, she was surprised to see a photograph of another man she recognized as the one her mother had hoped to marry, but could not. (He was already engaged when they met.) Her mother married someone else, and lived with him for fifty years; but behind her husband's picture, she kept her true love.

Things do not always work out the way we want. You may think this man's life with you would be the best for him, but if *he* doesn't see it that way, it isn't going to happen.

Desire blinds. The first requisite for receiving true guidance is to be inwardly detached. Even if you feel your longing is coming from a source greater than yourself, I would be careful about calling that God's will.

You can have strong desires and still be inwardly surrendered to God. That combination will leave you at peace, no matter how things turn out. While it may not be easy, you really have no other choice.

Be honest with God, as you have been. State your desire. But at the end of the prayer, say with as much sincerity as you can muster, "Thy will, not mine, be done."

From childhood, I have had a deep desire to be happy. Whenever I found myself in an unhappy state, I did my utmost to extricate myself as quickly as possible. To change a misery-making attitude to a positive one—or to let go of a desire that could never be fulfilled—was seldom easy. Still, adapting to what *is* always seemed preferable to clinging to what I merely *hoped* would be.

As I grew, I was surprised to discover how many people preferred to suffer, rather than face the need, and muster the energy, to change—exactly where you seem to be caught.

How many times will you throw yourself against the brick wall of unrequited love in the hope that this time it will turn into an open door? At some point you will see your present pain is greater than the imagined misery of letting go. *When* is up to you.

Have faith in God's will. If He wants you to be with this man, you could move to the other side of the world, and he would still find you. And if it isn't in your divine best interest, you could hover around him the rest of your life, and it still wouldn't draw him to you.

Once the heart has been given, it is hard to take it back. So instead of trying to rid yourself of the desire for him, concentrate rather on bringing into your life positive realities to fill the space where you hoped he would be.

What good things would happen if you and he were together? What activities would you enjoy? How would it change your consciousness? Some things depend on his being there, but not all.

Were he your partner, would you be more socially active, develop new friendships, be kinder? Start doing now everything you would if you *were* together.

I am in love with a man who doesn't love me.

In this way, the positive results you hope for in the relationship can manifest without it. Not only will this make your life more interesting, it will also get you out of limbo.

If, in the end, your original desire turns out to be God's will, you will have made yourself a better person while waiting. And if he never comes to you in the way you hope, you will still be a happier person, instead of a disappointed and lonely one. ❧

What does it mean in meditation to have an empty mind?

Many articles about meditation praise the idea; others say it is dangerous, not only in meditation, but also when induced by drugs or alcohol. They say having an empty mind can lead to possession by disincarnate entities. What is true?

K RIYA YOGA is the meditation I practice. I came to it early, and it has never ceased to inspire me, so I've not explored any other way. I've met many people from other traditions, so I'm familiar with the idea of empty mind meditation, but I've never tried it. So I'll speak from the point of view of Kriya.

The Sanskrit language specializes in describing states of consciousness. It has exact words for subtle realities. Other languages have not focused on the inner world to the same extent. In spiritual teachings, non-Sanskrit words are often defined by the traditions that use them, and are not consistent from one path to another. *Empty mind* is a good example.

In the Kriya tradition, this is not a positive concept. In other traditions, it is the heart of the practice. Maybe the disagreement is on principle; maybe it is just semantics.

In Kriya, the emphasis is on devotion and willpower. If by *empty*, one means passive, that is definitely not desirable. If *empty* means the absence of restless preoccupations, that is different. *Still* and *focused* are the words we use in Kriya. *Focused* requires something to focus on, and is therefore the opposite of empty. The difference is more than semantics.

The challenge in meditation is to let go of tension without lowering one's energy level—to relax and still the mind and body, without falling asleep. The energy habitually directed outward is used to hold oneself in an expanded state of inner awareness.

The biggest obstacle to emptying the mind is that *Nature abhors a vacuum.* Nothing *stays* empty. If one force is removed, another will rush to fill the void.

Master explains in *Autobiography of a Yogi* that thoughts are not individually rooted. Our minds are like radios, receiving programs from streams of consciousness to which we are attuned. We *identify* with our individual ego, but in truth we are part of a greater reality.

Some meditation methods make no reference to greater realities and avoid the idea of God altogether, offering what they call *non-deistic* spiritual practices. Kriya, by contrast, is all about God.

God is one of those words, though, where the meaning varies according to who uses it. *Satchidananda* is the Sanskrit equivalent preferred by Kriya yogis: *ever-existing, ever-conscious, ever-new Bliss.*

In Kriya, we empty the mind of its usual contents by concentrating on a greater reality. Whether Light, Guru, Divine Mother, or the Formless Infinite, it is definitely something other than emptiness. For the Kriya yogi, meditation is receptivity to higher realities, not a state of mind we create on our own.

The danger of an empty mind is twofold. The first is that, in trying to become empty, one may become passive and low-energy instead—no recipe for success in any endeavor. Meditation is outside the realm of everyday experience, but still governed by common sense.

The second, as you have read, is possible possession by disincarnate entities. It does happen. If you vacate your mind, someone else may move in.

No sincere teacher would recommend a practice either doomed to fail, or dangerous—so I assume the words *empty mind* in the traditions that use them mean something other than what I am talking about here.

Alcohol and drugs lessen your ability to control yourself. They blur your focus and weaken your will. Marijuana, for example, makes trivial things seem profound. Minor stimulation brings exaggerated pleasure. The *munchies,* for example—delight in eating far greater than usual—are seen as a happy side-effect of marijuana use.

Habitual users rely on getting drunk or high as the way to enjoy life. They fail to see that will power and expanded awareness alone—not intoxication—lead to lasting fulfillment.

Disincarnate beings are people who died so attached to material experiences that their progression through the astral world, and eventually into another physical body, has been derailed by a consuming desire to repossess what they feel has been unfairly taken away. They may also be seeking power over others.

These ghosts gather around places where people drink and take drugs, hoping for a chance to slip into a physical form not their own, either for the duration of the substance-induced stupor—or longer, if blank-minded passivity has become that person's habit. Such beings are normally held at bay by the fact that a body is fully occupied by the person rightfully possessing it.

Many dastardly deeds are committed under the influence of alcohol or drugs. Afterwards, those responsible may not remember anything, nor have any idea why they did such things. Sometimes it may be mild-altering substances giving a person's subconscious free rein. But an entity also could literally have used his body. The body's rightful owner would be responsible for putting himself in that position, but his lack of connection to the crime could be sincere.

We are not talking about an occasional absentminded moment, but habitual unwillingness to participate in one's own life.

As dreadful as all this sounds, it is not something most people have to worry about. The rightful order is usually preserved. You incarnate in a body, and are the sole occupant for the duration.

Meditation, practiced with willpower, following a method provided by a true guru, unequivocally slams the door against intrusion. The practice attunes you to a higher consciousness that can and will protect you, not only when meditating, but everywhere in your life. ❧

Sometimes in meditation I feel afraid.

I long to have deep experiences, but when they come, I draw back. How can I overcome this fear of going into the unknown divine realm?

*M*EDITATION STATES ARE SUBTLE, so let me begin by drawing a parallel with experiences more easily understood.

Before I got married, I had never traveled outside the United States. I didn't even have a passport. My husband, by contrast, loved to travel. He had already spent six months in Europe, and a month in India. After we got married, his karma trumped my stay-at-home ways.

At first, I was sometimes anxious being in a foreign country. We only know English; and thirty years ago, when we began to travel, English was less universal.

I worried about breaking cultural taboos, and finding myself surrounded by angry natives shouting at me in some strange tongue. Just for fun, God manifested a few of my fears.

We were in Athens. It was my first trip—our honeymoon. We liked to walk, and had been wandering around the city. It was late, and we decided to take a taxi back to the hotel.

The driver took a circuitous route to increase the fare, nearing the hotel several times before veering off again. I joke that I always know what I think, usually know what I feel, but rarely know where I am! So he fooled me completely.

David, however, saw exactly what was going on. When he protested, the driver brushed him off. When we finally got where we were going, David offered the appropriate fare and refused to budge when the driver pointed to the meter demanding more.

Communication was rough. The driver knew some English; we knew not a word of Greek.

We had gotten out of the cab and were standing in the street having what quickly escalated into a major disagreement. A crowd gathered, all contributing loudly—in Greek, of course—and pretty soon real life matched my imagined scenario.

I wasn't enjoying it; but at the same time, neither was it so bad! The fear was much worse than the reality. The crowd was exuberant, but not menacing. Still, I would have paid the fare and put an end to it. David stood his ground. The man was a bully. David was not inclined to give in.

Finally, in a brilliant conversation-stopper, the driver reached over, removed from David's face the prescription glasses he always wore, carefully folded them, got into his cab, and shut the door.

Within a few seconds David realized we had lost, and paid what was now ransom to get his glasses back.

The point is, meditation at first can seem like a foreign country, where the customs are unfamiliar, and we don't speak the language. In fact, we are *going* home, not *leaving* it. Still, we have grown up in exile. We are children of the King, living in the servants' quarters. The palace and its ways seem strange.

It is no surprise that you feel nervous, just as I was on that trip. Now, three decades and a few dozen trips later, I know people everywhere are the same. Why be nervous merely because language and customs vary?

When I asked Swamiji once about a confusing meditation experience, he said, "Don't be afraid, you'll get used to it."

"I'm not afraid," I said, but the tension in my voice gave me away. *You'll get used to it,* was good advice and proved true.

Don't compound your difficulty by worrying about it. Sure, you could analyze the ego, and your desire to maintain control, but why bother? It will only make matters worse.

One reason I weathered the Athens experience so well is because I was not alone.

Nor are we alone when we meditate. God and Guru are our constant companions. Inner worlds may be foreign to us, but they are the Guru's natural home. We have a local guide who knows the terrain, and speaks the dialect.

In the Bible it says, "Perfect love casts out all fear." Be like a little child placing your tiny hand in Father's grip—and do so *before* anxiety sets in.

If fear still overtakes you, cast yourself onto Divine Mother's lap. Curl up like a child. Feel Her arms around you.

I first went to India in 1986, as part of a pilgrimage called "In the Footsteps of Paramhansa Yogananda." We visited many of the places made holy by Master's presence, including his childhood home at 4 Garpar Road in Kolkata, where his nephew, Harekrishna Ghosh, was still living. We returned to the house many times over the next twenty years, gradually coming to know more and more members of Master's family.

Sheffli was Master's niece, Harekrishna's younger sister. Both of them met Master when he returned to India in 1935. Harekrishna was fifteen, and had almost adult memories of that visit; Sheffli was only three, and doesn't remember it at all, but has heard from older relatives many stories of how she related to Master, and how he responded to her.

She was utterly entranced by him. Whenever she saw Master, she would run to his side, cling to his leg, or climb onto his lap. Master returned her affection, and kept her close to him whenever possible.

Once the whole family was going to a movie. Sheffli was too young to go; but when they tried to separate her from Master, she cried. Master lifted Sheffli to his chest, buttoned his coat around her, and smuggled her in. While others watched the movie, she lay with her head against his heart.

My first response when I heard this story was, "What a waste! To have met Master only once, and be too young to remember!" But as I reflected, I saw the blessing. With the confidence of a child that she was welcome, and that her love would be returned, Sheffli gave herself to Master. Would that all disciples could love so freely! Her body was young, but her soul was ageless. The mind forgets, but the soul remembers.

"Suffer little children to come unto me, for of such is the Kingdom of God."

Since then, I have often visualized myself as a child clinging to Master's leg, climbing onto his lap, resting against his heart with his coat buttoned over me. Ah, bliss!

We are children of God, and as such have both a right and a duty to surrender completely, not only to His guidance, but also to His protective love.

In God's own home, under the protection of a Self-realized guru, what harm could befall us? "Perfect love casts out fear." ❧

In meditation I doze off and start dreaming instead.

Another problem is when I close my eyes to meditate, I see a densely-dotted, moving pattern. I feel as if I am seeing noise. This is all very distracting.

*M*EDITATING AND FALLING ASLEEP are more closely related than you might think. And certainly closer than we want them to be!

There are three states of consciousness: subconscious sleep, ordinary wakefulness, and superconscious meditation. We tend to picture these in linear sequence, from least to most aware. Sleep, then, is nicely separated from meditation by the waking state.

In fact, all three intersect at what you might call the horizon line of awareness.

Meditation and sleep share certain obvious characteristics. Both involve keeping the body still, withdrawing from the senses, and letting go of thoughts. The all-important difference is that sleep is a state of *decreased* energy and awareness, whereas meditation is an enormous *increase*.

In meditation classes, I draw a diagram to illustrate the relationship between the three states of consciousness. A child's printed version of a capital Y lying on its side, with the straight line pointing to the left connecting to the V opening on the right.

The leftmost point of that straight line is the state of being fully awake in ordinary consciousness. When you decide to sleep or meditate, you travel along that straight line to the right, closing down body, mind, and senses, until you reach the point where all three lines intersect.

There you have a choice. The side of the V that slopes downward represents the subconscious. Keep on decreasing your energy, and you will roll effortlessly into sleep.

The side of the V that slopes upward represents superconsciousness. If, after withdrawing from the conscious level, you *increase* rather than decrease your energy, you will rise into meditation. One reason meditation is challenging is that the increased energy is neither mental nor physical. It is more subtle. We don't create it; we open and receive it. It is always there, and accessible, but we are not in the habit of tuning into it.

Sometimes your meditation starts strong, and you feel yourself rising. If, after a time, your energy wanes, you'll find your consciousness beginning to sink. When it reaches the point where the three levels meet, you may suddenly stand up and go back to wakefulness. Or, if your energy keeps going down, you fall asleep.

Each state of consciousness has a corresponding position of the eyes. Watch a sleepy child, and you'll see his eyes drooping. In the ordinary waking state, the eyes are level, looking straight out at the world. In superconsciousness, the eyes are uplifted, looking into, or at least drawn toward, the light at the spiritual eye.

If in meditation you feel yourself drifting toward subconsciousness, or suddenly realize you have fallen asleep, just lifting your eyes will help pull you out of that state.

Then, with eyes uplifted, increase your energy through one or more of the methods taught in Kriya, or whatever path of Self-realization you follow. Pray for yourself or others, chant, repeat a mantra, say an affirmation, visualize your chosen image of God at the spiritual eye. Call on God to "Reveal Thyself! Take me into Thy Light." These will help lift you back into superconsciousness. By repeated, concentrated effort, eventually you will break the habit of associating stillness with sleep. Falling asleep in meditation will cease to be a problem.

The time and place of your meditation is also something to consider. Perhaps you are meditating too late at night. Try right after work, before dinner. The Energization Exercises, as taught in Kriya, are also a great aid. Do them outside, or in front of an open window.

When you meditate, wrap yourself in a blanket, so you can keep the room cool and fresh. Don't sit on the bed. Have a dedicated chair or cushion—better still, a specific place in your house. Just as your bed, sheets, and pillows are permeated with subconscious vibrations, your meditation space will become saturated with superconscious energy.

As for the visual noise, it is a bit of a circle. The moving pattern disrupts concentration, and also results from lack of concentration. The solution is to persevere.

Meditation is both a science and an art. The science is the techniques; the art is being creative in using them. Since the distraction in this case is visual, maybe an alternate visualization is the answer. Picture the spiritual eye, or the face of a saint, or the eyes of Master as you see them in photos.

Since you also describe this as noise, perhaps you want to chant, mentally or aloud, and in this way dissipate the restlessness causing the image. Experiment, and see what works.

Consider practical questions. Is there too much light? Can you darken the window, blow out the candle, or cover your eyes?

Most important, don't give up. Any effort to meditate, no matter how distracted, will bring great benefit. When we first start, the mind can be compared to a runaway horse. Early efforts to concentrate are comparable to the first tentative tug on the reins, when the horse still has the bit in his teeth. It seems nothing is happening, but eventual mastery of that horse begins with the first feeble, "Whoa, horsey!"

It is the same with the mind and senses. It doesn't matter how far you are from where you aspire to be. The only way to get there is right from where you presently stand. ❧

Two "karmic bombs" went off this week.

Nuclear bombs that will change my life forever. The teachings say: "Pray. Accept. Go with the flow." But I don't want to! I'm sad, angry, and filled with negativity. I took Kriya initiation a few months ago, and some people warned me, "Watch out! After initiation your life will fall apart!" I dismissed that as ridiculous, but now I wonder.

 $\mathcal{T}$HE EGO SEES LIFE in terms of *pleasure* and *ease*. The definition of these words varies from person to person. Mountain climbing is exhilarating to some, terrifying to others; raucous music is delightful or excruciating, depending on your point of view.

From a spiritual perspective, though, what the ego thinks is irrelevant. Sister Gyanamata, Master's most highly advanced woman disciple, taught: "It doesn't matter what happens to us; what matters is what we become through our experiences."

People often think the proof of God's love is all the nice things He does for us. We give Him our prayers, meditation, and a little money. In return He gives us a job, a nice home, and a parking place whenever needed. But thinking of God like this makes us little more than customers, scanning the shelves for bargains.

Being a devotee is not a business deal. You may have drawn up a contract listing the conditions God must meet if He wants your love, but only *you* signed it. We are His children, not His clients. He is our Divine Mother, and like any good mother is going to help us realize our full potential.

On the first day of kindergarten, a child may feel abandoned by the mother who has loved and protected him, but she has done nothing of the kind. It would be cruel *not* to send him to school.

So it is with Divine Mother. We have the power within "to stand unshaken amidst the crash of breaking worlds!" This is our destiny, and nothing less will satisfy Her.

In a sense, Kriya *is* responsible, because taking initiation is a way of telling God, "I want to expand my consciousness." He heard, and is helping you realize that aspiration. That your first response has been negative, speaks of much to learn.

External conditions are temporary. Whether through attrition, natural progression, or karmic bombs, everything eventually becomes something else. Even the body you cherish is temporary. Only consciousness is eternal.

The limitations to your consciousness revealed by these changed conditions were always lurking behind the comfortable life you had. That you were unaware of them did not free you from their influence. The bliss your heart longs to experience will never be yours until all limitations are gone. Be grateful! Now you can start dissolving them.

As for your Kriya practice *causing* these difficulties, it's unlikely you could generate enough power in a few months to change your destiny! People blame Kriya for their troubles, hoping that if they stop practicing, things will revert back to normal.

Bombs like these take years—or lifetimes—to build, then detonate. If a gifted astrologer had looked at your horoscope the day you were born, he probably could have predicted precisely when.

Kriya is your haven. It was God's grace that the bombs didn't go off sooner. With Kriya, you can access your true Self, untouched by mere outward shifting.

Karmic bombs force you to choose: Cling to God, or run from Him.

"Poor me," the wounded heart says. "I'm too sad to meditate today." You avoid spiritual company. "I don't want to bring others down." This is not wisdom. It is negativity protecting itself.

Darkness cannot be dissipated by beating at it with a stick. Whether that stick is tears, anger, or shame, none of it will work. Darkness disappears in the presence of Light. Seek Light every way you can, and you will soon find yourself standing firm in faith and love for God. 〜

How does karma get from one incarnation to the next?

Can one person's karma be determined by another person's will? If a wife dies still attached to her husband, but the husband is not so attached to her, will her desire alone cause them to marry again in a future life?

$\mathcal{K}$ARMA IS ALWAYS FAIR. It is a divine law, the impersonal working out of cause and effect. Since most people have forgotten huge chunks of the life they are now living, and remember nothing at all of past lives, the absolute fairness of karma is rarely evident to those most directly involved.

Karma is *unlearned lessons*. Everything happens for a reason, and always for one's own highest good. If you have nothing to learn from a certain experience, it will not come to you.

Those compelled to face extremely difficult circumstances eventually realize, "They made me who I am. I wouldn't have it any other way." Ideally, understanding comes in the same incarnation the causative events occur. But even if it has to wait for the expanded perspective of the astral plane, or some future lifetime, we *will* understand.

Karma, reincarnation, and the *chakras*—the subtle energy centers in the spine—are one integrated system.

With every thought, deed, or desire, we act according to our perception of reality, and in what we believe to be our own best interest. Everyone is motivated to seek happiness and escape pain. Even if our response turns out to be misguided, *it always seems like a good idea at the time.*

Let's say a man treats you unfairly, and you respond with anger. Revenge, you believe, will increase your happiness and reduce your pain. This is one perception of reality. If your response is compassion, and a concern for the karmic consequences to him, that reflects another.

When Jesus was crucified, rather than being angry with those who condemned him, he prayed: "Father, forgive them, for they know not what they do." In such an extreme circumstance, to forget oneself in favor of others shows a God-united view of reality.

All of us eventually reach that level. It is our inescapable destiny. The difference between our present consciousness and that of a Christ is the measure of how much karma we still have to work out.

Every level of reality has its own vibration. Each of the chakras, from the base of the spine to the point between the eyebrows, represents a gradually ascending vibration, from material to spiritual, from self-affirming to Self-realized.

Though our human mind quickly forgets what we have done, the energy passing through us does not dissipate. To the extent we are ego-identified, our actions remain bound to us. All are recorded in our chakras, corresponding to the level of consciousness from which the action emanated. These trapped vibrations make whirlpools of energy called vrittis.

The chakras are not physical. They are a causal and astral phenomenon, around which the body forms. When the physical body dies, the chakras remain intact and move with the astral body into that world. The pattern of vrittis determines which astral universe we are drawn to and, eventually, the nature of our next physical incarnation.

Modern science confirms what great yogis have long asserted: Matter is an illusion. Everything in this universe is a vibration of energy. The implication of this is just beginning to dawn: *Magnetism,* acting upon the *energy nature of the universe,* is the force that shapes our destiny.

Magnetism is not a matter of opinion, whim, or even the will of God as something separate from oneself. It is an impersonal fact, the accumulated result of everything we ourselves have done.

Let's say a person is attached to money. Behind that attachment is the belief that money equals power, and power will increase happiness. The energy expended on that belief makes a vritti, which is stored in the chakra corresponding to that perception of reality.

In fact, money is not the *source* of power or happiness; it only *appears* so. This common belief limits one's consciousness to a level below that of a Christ. The vritti lurks in the appropriate chakra as an unlearned lesson, a karma still to be worked out, and generates magnetism, which attracts—in some incarnation—the experiences needed to learn that lesson, and understand reality on a higher plane.

In terms of human relationships, the same principle applies. If a woman thinks happiness depends on having a particular man as her husband, what gets recorded in her chakra is the desire for a certain ego-based love. Even if the love is unselfish, it is still ego-based to the extent she limits it to this one expression.

The wife's attachment to one soul as the only person she can love is a misunderstanding indeed. Whether that wife will again have that man as her husband, though, depends not only on the vrittis in her chakras, but also on the vrittis in his.

If he longs for her in the way she longs for him, that could draw them together. If he despises her, or fears being close to her again, that could draw them together as well. If he feels sorry for her, and worries about her wellbeing—if he lacks faith that God will look after her—that could do it.

If, on the other hand, the wife has lessons to learn, but the husband's unlearned lessons are not a match for hers, she still has to work out the karma—but with someone else now, not him.

The chakras create a pattern of energy reflecting a particular perception of reality. For her, a too-personal definition of love, and the mistaken belief that she cannot open her heart except to him.

Her desire, and the connection between them, may cause them to meet in a future life. If he refuses to marry her, will rejection turn her love to anger, and from anger to hate? In this way, close relationships, too narrowly defined or poisoned by attachment, seesaw repeatedly over incarnations.

The more receptive we are to higher levels of awareness, the more quickly we learn. The more we rebel, the longer it takes.

Can one soul force karma onto another? No, there has to be a corresponding resonance, but it can be subtle. That is why honest introspection, prayer, and self-offering to God are needed for us to become free.

It is disheartening to think how many lifetimes it could take to resolve even one relationship. Multiply that by all our relationships in all lifetimes, and Eternity itself would not be enough. Fortunately, the Creator has planted within us a shortcut, which everyone eventually finds.

Karma is not physical; it is patterns of energy, vrittis in the chakras. The shortcut is to work directly with that energy *before* it manifests. Dissolve the vritti, and you dissolve the karma.

This is not magic. It takes determined effort. The same energy it would take to live through the karma still has to be expended, but inwardly.

Kriya Yoga is one name for this ancient method of dissolving karma. A complete inhalation and exhalation, circulated through the chakras in a particular way, equals one year of right living, without the peril inherent in everyday life that, while dissolving one vritti, you may inadvertently create a host of others.

You are in charge of your destiny. You can proceed, as most do, with the hit-or-miss approach of facing karma as it manifests. Or you can go inward and take the "airplane route to God." ✑

Why do bad things happen to good people?

A friend of ours literally hit a karmic bump in the road, crashing his motor scooter and seriously fracturing his leg. For weeks he was confined to bed, in intense pain, and dependent on his wife for "everything relating to the material plane." He is a good person and has been meditating for years. Still, such a bad thing happened!

*A*BOUT TWELVE TIMES over the course of twenty years, David and I have led pilgrimage tours to many of the holy places described in *Autobiography of a Yogi*. We filled one bus, thirty people, mostly devotees, mostly Americans who had never before been to India or any developing nation.

Due to poverty and overpopulation, you see things in India you don't see here. Families living on the sidewalk, deformed beggars, trinket vendors, who follow you for blocks, refusing to take no for an answer.

(In India's defense, prosperity is on the rise, and much of what we saw then is not so common now.)

Some people choose not to visit developing nations; they fear they won't be able to cope with the poverty. Many of our pilgrims were concerned, but that didn't keep them from coming.

Their reactions varied. Some adapted effortlessly; others were forever ill at ease. After a while, a certain pattern emerged.

Whether or not a person could be at peace with the conditions there was usually a reflection of how calmly he could accept *in his own life* that suffering is an inevitable stage on the path to Bliss.

In other words, as Master put it, "An easy life is not a victorious one."

From the ego's point of view, the purpose of life is comfort. America is particularly dedicated to this "ideal." This is not, however, God's perspective. What He wants for us is Bliss. The ease of the moment means nothing to Him compared to Eternity.

By contrast, we are like children. Our perspective is so limited. When unpleasant things happen, we rebel at the unfairness of life. In the heat of the moment, we rarely remember that difficult experiences teach us important lessons we couldn't learn any other way.

A mother told me that from the time her daughter was an infant, the family always said grace before meals, ending with, "AUM. Peace. Amen."

When the child turned three, she was finally able to ask a question that had long puzzled her. "Mommy, why do we only bless the peas and almonds?" All those years, she had heard: "AUM. Peas. Almonds."

Here's another example, of the "Gospel According to Children."

A little girl came home from Sunday school, and announced, "Don't worry, Mommy, the quilt is coming!" The mother accepted this news graciously, but later called the teacher.

Turned out the lesson had been, "Be of good cheer, the Lord will send you the Comforter."

It's all in your point of view.

Karma is neither good nor bad. It simply is. It is energy in motion that must be resolved. Karma is like waves on the surface of the vast ocean of consciousness. Every upward-moving wave is balanced by a trough. In the end it all comes to zero. No matter how high the waves or how deep the troughs, the overall level of the ocean remains unchanged.

We call karma *bad* if it makes us uncomfortable, and *good* if it brings us pleasure. How foolish! The only *good* karma, in the final sense, is having no karma at all. Finishing the game.

Resting at last in the great Ocean of Spirit. Dissolving the ego, and becoming *jivan-mukta*—freed while living.

Yes, the scooter accident made our friends uncomfortable—he by confinement, she by having to give up everything else to take care of him. She wryly titled her blog entry on the subject: "Never Say: I Need a Break."

The ego will not give way to the divine merely because we say please. It takes courage, will power, and determination. God is on our side, and sends us just what we need. No matter how challenging, whatever comes is a gift, and can rightly be called *good karma.* ❧

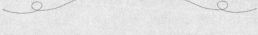

An ugly divorce has devolved into guerilla warfare.

My ex-wife uses our kids to get to me. My heart fills with fear and a terrible anger, which only adds to the strain on the children. For their sake, as well as mine, how can I overcome my negative feelings?

*S*O SEE YOUR FAMILY IMPLODE is difficult indeed. It can't be easy to stay calm in the midst of it. Still, what choice is there? You can't control your ex-wife's behavior. You can't live your children's lives for them. This karma is theirs too, a reality that has to be faced.

With karma like this, our first impulse is rarely, "Let me face it head on!" Especially when those we love are being hurt. Instead we try to make it go away.

The Ananda Festival of Light includes an allegory about the spiritual awakening of a little bird. The bird disregards divine law, and suffers. Even when given wise advice, it refuses to listen. Instead of adapting to life as it is, it makes up its own rules. This stage in its evolution is called *The Revolt*.

Problem is, it doesn't work. Truth always wins. In the allegory, the little bird repeatedly loses everything it has. Still, it clings to false ideas. Finally, after much suffering, it surrenders and embraces *The Quest*, wanting now to understand a greater reality.

No matter how unjust your present situation seems, remember: *Karma is always fair*. Rebelling did not serve the little bird, nor will it serve you. This is hard to accept—unbearably so when your children are involved.

No spiritual progress is possible, though, until you take this truth to the marrow of your bones: *Karma is always fair*. There will be no resolution until you advance from *The Revolt* to *The Quest*.

Whatever is happening now is the result of wrong attitudes and actions in the past, whether in this life or those long forgotten. You and your children set energy in motion. The circle is completing itself.

"Who in their right mind would inflict this kind of suffering on oneself and one's children?" you may well ask. Whatever you did that started this karma is not something you now embrace. Or do you? You speak of fear and anger. What motivates your wife? Would it be fair to say that she, too, is compelled by the same emotions tormenting you?

Karma is unlearned lessons. To respond to anything in life with fear and anger means you have much left to learn. Perhaps you have grown past retaliating in kind, but unresolved energy lingers. Your reaction makes that clear.

Either learn the lessons now, or face the karma again in some future incarnation.

That you are appealing to a spiritual source for help means you have learned a great deal already. God is *always* the solution. Wisdom now is to do your best to learn whatever lessons remain, and to help your children do the same.

What might those lessons be? It is not easy to pierce the veil between lives and see how the past is playing out in the present. If you can find someone compassionate and wise who can read past lives, consider a session. Sometimes knowing these influences helps us persevere in the right way.

Above all, have faith that God is in charge, even in a situation so far removed from what you want to accept as God's will.

I suspect there is little you can do to resolve this directly. There are no laws against wrong attitude, which is what your ex-wife is expressing in spades (and drawing you into as well). The only solution is on the level of consciousness.

You have to become a world-class athlete of consciousness. The situation with your ex-wife and children is your gold medal event. Train like an Olympian.

"I can't afford the luxury of a single, negative thought," one of my friends said, after developing cancer. She was already the sweetest woman I knew, but still she saw room for improvement.

All the attitudes that pull us to pieces in the major challenges of our lives are expressed, too, in the lesser ones. We don't notice that we are responding with anger, because nothing seems at stake. Railing at a bad driver, being annoyed with a roommate who leaves dishes in the sink, or getting mad at the weather may not seem connected to your ex-wife, but it is.

Anger is a habit. Practice when it's easier to resist. Then when the big challenge comes you'll have the strength to stay centered.

Consciousness is the only weapon you have in this guerilla war. The good news is that consciousness is everything! Not only will it change your experience, it is also the primary influence you can have on your children, and the way ultimately to resolve this situation.

When a person no longer gets the result he wants from the action he is taking, he loses interest in repeating it. Your ex-wife has gotten to you through your kids. You need to find a depth of God-knowing that nullifies her tactics.

Your children, seeing your calmness even in the face of extreme provocation, may even be inspired to follow your example. Whether sooner or later, it *will* have a positive effect on them.

Right consciousness is the one gift you can give, and the most precious one of all. ~&

Are all astral worlds beautiful?

I've heard that some souls are confined to "astral slums."
If we choose our own fate, why would anyone choose
that? Is that how karma works?

*J*F YOU ARE RESPONSIBLE for raising a child, you must teach him that actions have consequences. Merely telling him is usually not enough. The best teacher is experience.

Between the spoken word "hot," and the way it feels on a child's hand, there is a world of difference. A mother walks a fine line between protecting her child, and letting him have the experiences he needs to grow. Sometimes touching the hot stove, if it is the only way he'll learn.

Our Divine Mother has the responsibility of raising us from ego-delusion into perfect Bliss. Whether in the physical or the non-physical worlds, She watches over us. A human mother guides her child for one incarnation; Divine Mother guides us for eternity.

The consequences of our actions do not dissipate merely because our bodies die. Consciousness continues at whatever level of realization we have achieved. Though we think of each incarnation and the time in between as separate events, in fact, they are one continuous flow. Birth and death, and life in the astral world, are like walking from one room to another. A few things change, but not as many as we imagine.

The continuing individual consciousness is called in Sanskrit the *jiva*. It is similar to the word *soul*, but more exact. Swamiji defined jiva as "the infinite limited to, and identified with, a body." The body referred to is physical, astral, and causal, so the consciousness is consistent in all three worlds.

Master says that in order to transcend delusion completely, we must first experience every form delusion can take, otherwise we will still think happiness can be found somewhere other than in our divine Self. That thought keeps us from merging with God.

Think about some hard lesson you learned this lifetime. No doubt your friends warned you. Did you listen? Or did you understand only *after* experiencing the consequences of your wrong actions?

Experience is the best, in fact, the only true teacher.

If you are no longer drawn to being a murderer, Master says that in previous lifetimes you tried murder, and learned it does not bring the fulfillment you seek. Hopefully, that delusion is now forever crossed off your list. Look around, though, and observe others still learning this.

Think now of delusions less dramatic, ones that still have a hold on you. Close friends may not be bound by these at all. Their freedom may be as much a mystery to you as your bondage is to them.

Unfortunately, when subtle delusions are involved, it takes more than one touch of a hot stove to persuade us a particular action is not in our best interest.

If a person behaves without concern for others, then finds himself after death living in an "astral slum," it may indeed be harsh, but is it inappropriate? If a child does something profoundly hurtful to others, should his mother just murmur, "Bad boy," and leave it at that?

If, because of the suffering the jiva endures in the "astral slum," he sees the error of his ways and resolves to live on a higher vibration, was living there a punishment or a perfect expression of Divine Mother's love?

How does a guru take on the karma of his disciples?

If he works it out on his own body, what happens after the guru dies? Can he no longer help them? If I want to help a friend, can I take on his karma?

$\mathcal{J}$HE KARMIC LAW of cause and effect has to be satisfied one way or another. "A spiritual superman," Master said, "is able to minimize his disciples' physical or mental burdens by sharing the karma of their past actions." Directing the energy through his own body is one of many ways a master can do this.

The crucifixion of Jesus is the best-known example of a guru physically taking on others' karma. Instead of *karma,* the churches use the word *sin,* but the meaning is the same. They are wrong, though, when they say his crucifixion settled everyone's destiny forever.

It was specifically for the benefit of his close disciples at that time. Soon after, on the day of Pentecost, they were lifted into a high state of consciousness. Master says this was because Jesus had worked out much of their karma on his own body.

The church *is* correct, however, in saying Jesus can still free us, though not through the pay-it-forward effect of his crucifixion. Rather it is through the power of his consciousness alone, there being no physical body now to absorb the energy.

High spiritual souls routinely experience medical conditions not caused by their own karma. In the last years of his life, Master had so much trouble with his knees that he often couldn't walk.

"Carry my body," he laughed, as the monks bore him up a flight of stairs, "and I will carry your souls."

In the course of writing the book, *Swami Kriyananda as We Have Known Him*, I asked Swamiji whether he also took on the karma of others. His illnesses were so unusual (and the cures, unpredictable) that this seemed the obvious explanation.

Usually Swamiji was quite forthcoming, especially when my purpose was to write about him. In this case, though, he talked all around the subject. Finally he said, "I've prayed to Master to help others any way I can," then added, "It's not up to me. It is for God to decide."

I remembered Swamiji telling us about Master having lunch with a few guests. One said casually, "I understand Dr. Lewis was your first disciple in this country."

Master became unexpectedly reserved. "That is what they say," he replied. Discipleship, Swamiji explained, was for Master "too sacred a subject to be treated lightly, even in casual conversation."

A guru taking on the karma of his disciples is a gift of such magnitude we cannot begin to fathom it. He must have not only the power to transfer the karma to himself, but also the wisdom to know when it is right to do so.

If we had the power to remove karma, in our blindness, we could blunder terribly. In the memoirs of a healer who became known as Peace Pilgrim, she describes some lessons she had to learn about when to make a person well, and when to leave the symptoms in place as a necessary learning.

Master many times exhorted his listeners to rise to seemingly unreachable heights. On the subject of assuming others' karma, though, he is silent.

"The metaphysical method of physical transfer of disease," Master explains in *Autobiography of a Yogi*, "is known to highly advanced yogis." Nowhere does he say, "Go and do likewise."

Taking on the karma of others may be the pinnacle of spiritual service, but even wandering at the mountain's base, we still have much to give.

Swamiji was in the hospital once, recovering from surgery. He woke in the middle of the night to see his nurse, also a devotee, meditating.

"I am too ill to do my kriyas," he said. "Could you do them for me?"

On another occasion, a devotee's birthday gift to Swamiji was doing her kriyas for his benefit. He was deeply touched. When another devotee was herself hospitalized, Swamiji said he would meditate for her.

By our selfless efforts, we *can* uplift one another spiritually. It is a more subtle expression of the way we help each other all the time: lending money, lifting heavy objects, being present when challenges must be faced. We may not be able to assume the karma of those we love, but we can mitigate its effect by adding our energy to theirs.

Karma is too complex to be shifted about casually, even with the best of intentions. Many a mother has prayed over her sick child, "Give this suffering to me." Rarely is that prayer answered. Only the greatest among us are allowed to help in this way. Still, it is just further up the spectrum of service we already provide. As Master said about enlightenment itself, "That will come." ❧

Is it bad karma to give up a baby for adoption?

What if the pregnancy is the result of rape? Would it be bad karma to give that baby away?

$\mathcal{C}$ ONCEPTION IS a joint venture, not only between the man and the woman, but also with the incoming soul. Compared to how often people have sex, conception is an infrequent occurrence. The karma of the incarnating soul is an essential part of the equation.

Giving up a child for adoption is not in itself bad karma. It depends on *why* the parents are doing it. Sometimes the mother decides alone, but the father also has responsibility. Most biologically mature men and women can conceive a child, but that doesn't mean they are able to raise one.

For a child conceived in violence, adoption would be an obvious choice. Terminating a pregnancy is a difficult decision, but rape is a time when it certainly could be considered.

Children conceived by people quite young are often better off raised by more mature adults. It might be good karma for teenagers to think first of the child's welfare, and not be swept away by emotion.

The incoming soul knows the conditions into which it is being born. Master says when the sperm and ovum unite, there is a flash of light in the astral world. Souls who are in tune with that light, and ready to reincarnate, respond to the possibility of entering that womb.

Obviously, the biological parents have karma with the incoming soul, otherwise it would not feel drawn to that particular flash. It is not unreasonable to think, though, that the karma might only be for the soul to obtain a physical body and that the joint karma of parents and child could end at birth.

The child's lifelong karma may be with the adopting family. Perhaps the biological parents will come back into the picture, but there is no reason they must.

Think how many times the soul incarnates in its long journey to Self-realization. Each time there is a mother and father, plus, perhaps, adoptive parents, stepparents, surrogates. We live through every permutation. Each has lessons to teach.

In truth, the "child" is not a child at all, but a soul. The body has age; the soul is ageless. A new incarnation does not mean a clean slate. The conditions of each birth are a perfect reflection of what that soul needs to progress spiritually, based on the accumulated karma of all the lives coming before.

Same for the mother and father. Conceiving a child they can't (or don't want to) raise is, for them, exactly the karma they need to learn whatever lesson is next.

The lessons and the learning are entirely personal. For one, it may be thinking first of the child's welfare. For another, it could be taking responsibility for one's own actions.

God is no tyrant. Often we do things without being aware of the repercussions. God reads the heart, not some chart of right and wrong behavior with appropriate rewards and punishments assigned to each. We do the best we can.

If later you understand you made a mistake, don't torture yourself. Look at it objectively. Accept responsibility, and resolve not to make that mistake again.

That is all God asks of us—that we don't give up, but keep trying and never lose faith in His all-merciful love. ❧

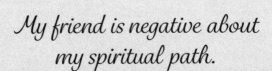

My friend is negative about my spiritual path.

I've had some great experiences since I started meditating—vibrations in the chakras, waking to the sound of AUM, increasing trust and love for God. At the same time, so much so fast makes me feel insecure. Is this normal? My friend says I'm fooling myself with all this talk of loving God. When I protest, she gets angry, so I have distanced myself from her. She says breaking our friendship is bad karma. What should I do?

*J*F YOU MOVED TO another country, you might enjoy the adventure, and at the same time feel insecure until you became familiar with the culture. Starting on the
spiritual path is much the same—delightful, and a step into
the unknown. Your experiences and your response to them are
normal.

The response of your friend is also common. She may be
genuinely concerned you are getting into something that won't
turn out well. Still, she is not showing much respect for your
judgment.

If she continues to negate these precious, new experiences,
why would you want to spend time with her? Newly emerging
love for God can too easily be quenched, or at least sullied, by
strong negativity.

Better not to gamble with your spiritual future—especially
since you are still a sapling, and like any young tree, need to
be protected from the elements while your trunk thickens and
your roots grow deep. Unfortunately, by her behavior, your
friend has forced a choice upon you.

To tell someone they are getting bad karma is no different
than a fundamentalist saying, "You will go to hell!" That is for
God to decide. The fate of others is not in our hands.

It is unfortunate your friend has decided to respond this
way. Some people feel threatened by others' spirituality. Perhaps inside she knows you have taken the higher path and
feels shamed by the contrast. Maybe she is jealous, because you

have Someone in your life who means more to you than her. She doesn't understand that God poses no threat.

If she continues to insult you, don't spend time with her, even in thought or prayer, since doing so may connect you to her negativity.

Tell Divine Mother that right now you are not able to be her friend. Let Her take over. If your friend changes, of course, welcome her back; but if she stays angry, keep your distance.

To accomplish anything in life means making choices— hard choices. Sad things happen along the way, like separation from a friend who doesn't understand.

The best way to be her friend is to do the right thing, which includes making sure her bad energy doesn't pull you down. Our spiritual progress is a blessing to those we love. Even if the egos of some disapprove, their souls rejoice.

My boyfriend thinks only the Catholic religion is true.

He no longer practices, but still thinks other ways are false, even sinful. He thinks my interest in Self-realization is silly, and hopes I'll grow out of it. I am just starting, and not very good at explaining it. How can I strengthen both my relationship with my boyfriend and my relationship with God?

*H*OW CAN I STRENGTHEN both relationships?" you ask; but the first question is, "Can it be done?"

Is this the first time you have noticed how narrow-minded your boyfriend is? Or is this just the first time it mattered? How many life changes have you been through together?

Whether his attitude will prove significant depends on how serious you are, and how persistent he is in his skepticism.

Here is a principle followed at Ananda that has served us well: *Where there is dharma, there is victory. Dharma* means right action, or more exactly, "that action which leads to greater awareness," especially of the divine within. "Victory" means the triumph of light over darkness, of happiness over sorrow.

Fulfillment comes when we adhere to high principles. If, to pacify your boyfriend, you hold back from God, you are not likely to find fulfillment in either relationship. What will happen if you don't grow out of this as your boyfriend hopes? You have a right to be concerned. It is difficult to make a life together when core values are not aligned.

But let's not get ahead of ourselves. Give him a chance to accept you. Even if he never embraces a more expansive path himself, the fact that it makes you happy may be enough. In the meantime, follow the advice of Jesus, and "Seek ye first the Kingdom of God. All these things shall be added unto you."

As for explaining the spiritual path to him, don't try too hard. Self-realization is subtle, and in the beginning it's more about feelings than concepts. Faced with skepticism, clear feeling evaporates. Words fail to express what you want to say. Even those on the path for years have trouble explaining it to someone unreceptive.

Be light-hearted ("Wow, that doesn't make sense, does it!"). If he points out obvious contradictions, don't get defensive ("I'll keep that in mind!"). Don't declare a commitment beyond what is sincere ("It's helping me right now. Let me just take it a step at a time, and see where it leads.").

You don't have to acquiesce to his doubts. Neither do you have to dismantle them. How well you handle this difference of opinion will tell you much about the way your future together may unfold. ❧

Dark aliens from other planets have interbred with Earthlings.

Much of the evil we see now is the result of alien invasion. Do you agree?

*U*FOs, interplanetary travel, or even colonization by beings from other planets—Master says all of this is not only possible, but has happened before, and will happen again.

A few of Master's disciples, living with him at Mt. Washington, wanted to visit Mt. Shasta, because they had heard ancient spiritual masters lived inside that mountain.

"There are no masters there," Master said. "There have been colonists, but no masters." Colonists from *where* one can only speculate. As for invasions from other planets, interbreeding, beings that feed on negative energy—all this could be true, but there are other explanations for what we see on Earth.

Creation's drama is the same everywhere. Whether on Earth, Mars, or planets yet to be discovered, the only "plot" in the universe is consciousness, confined by ego-based self-definitions, gradually freeing itself from all delusion. *Everything* is a manifestation of the divine, and *everything* seeks to return to its Source.

Some self-definitions are so far from the truth that they lead to hideous behavior. Look at the Chinese takeover of Tibet, Communism under Stalin, Nazis in Germany. You *could* explain these horrors in terms of alien invaders mating with humans to create an evil race. It would be comforting to explain such descents into madness as something other than what I believe them to be: the degraded potential of human consciousness.

No matter how degraded, no one is *inherently* evil. Darkness is not a separate reality. Such souls are utterly confused, though, as to the source of their own happiness.

Master states that before a soul attains liberation it experiments with *every possible alternative*. We don't learn from being told—only through experience. "Been there, done that" is exactly how it is. When we are no longer attracted to a certain action, it is because sometime in the past—in this life, or a previous one—we have drunk that cup to the dregs, and *know* it will not bring the fulfillment we seek.

It is almost impossible to get one's mind around that. To think we have been capable of the most ignorant behavior, the worst depravity, is disconcerting. It also speaks of a very long time before we achieve liberation. Why else, though, are we so certain that some things can never satisfy? We don't merely *believe*; we *know*.

"Will the people now on Earth be reborn here?" Master was once asked.

"No. When a soul returns from the astral to the material world, there are many planets available to it. Where it goes depends on its level of spiritual development."

Planets vary in the overall degree of enlightenment shown by their inhabitants. Earth right now is a mixture of darkness and light. It is some comfort to remember Master said we incarnate on the planet most appropriate for us—*spiritually*, that is, not just where it will be most pleasant.

The nature of a planet is determined by where it is in the cycle of *yugas* (long periods of ascending and descending consciousness), as determined by where that planet is in relation to the center of its galaxy. Great energy emanates from each galactic center. The closer a planet is to the source, the more enlightened its citizenry. Scientists are just beginning to veri-

Dark aliens from other planets have interbred with Earthlings.

fy something sages have long known—that solar systems orbit around their galactic centers.

A yuga cycle doesn't play out in one or two generations. On Earth, it takes 24,000 years—12,000 years ascending, as the elliptical orbit brings our solar system closer to the center, then 12,000 years descending, as it moves away.

There are four yugas, ascending and descending. Kali Yuga (the least enlightened) is the *Age of Matter*. Dwapara Yuga is the *Age of Energy*. Then comes Treta Yuga, the *Age of Thought*, followed by Satya Yuga, the *Age of Spirit*. At the nadir of each cycle, Kali Yuga descending is followed immediately by Kali Yuga ascending. At the apex, Satya Yuga ascending is followed by Satya Yuga, descending.

The four yugas vary in length; the more enlightened are longer. Satya Yuga is roughly four times as long as Kali Yuga. Each yuga is the same length both ascending and descending. Between each, there are 200-800 years of transition before the yuga proper begins—the longer the yuga, the longer the transition.

The nadir of the present cycle happened in 500 A.D. At that point, Kali Yuga descending shifted to Kali Yuga ascending. The transition into Dwapara Yuga ascending began in 1700, with the yuga proper beginning in 1900—explaining the exponential expansion of consciousness and technology the world has seen since.

The news, however, is not all good. Dwapara is more advanced than Kali, but it is not heaven on Earth, and the beginnings of each yuga are always unsettled times. We have the wherewithal to blow ourselves to bits, but not the moral clarity to keep from doing so. We draw great wealth from the Earth, but lack the generosity to share it equally.

Even in Treta Yuga, people go to war. It is far from the full expression of man's spiritual potential. Space travel is common, making *Star Trek* a reality—planets and species getting all mixed up in war and peace.

When you look forward and back at society through the yuga lens, a great deal that is otherwise bewildering makes sense. For more, read *The Yugas*, by Joseph Selbie and David Steinmetz.

No matter how interesting, though, the yugas remain a physical phenomenon, a mere backdrop for creation's real drama: The soul's effort to free itself from delusion and return to its home in God.

Great masters incarnate in every yuga. Jesus was born at nearly the lowest point of Kali Yuga descending. He was completely Self-realized, and many of his disciples were highly advanced. It was the right time and place for all of them. Christianity was one of the reasons civilization was not lost when Earth crossed the nadir of that cycle.

Whatever happens in the world, our individual assignments are always the same: to love, serve, and meditate. Only in this way will our divine destinies be fulfilled. ☙

I have lost interest in sex, but my wife has not.

For her it is a sustaining part of marriage. She isn't on the spiritual path, and sees no reason to be celibate. At first, I could tolerate moderation, but now I find it hard to oblige her at all. Otherwise, our marriage and family life is perfect. How can I be loyal both to my marriage and my spiritual practice?

A MARRIED DEVOTEE in the same situation asked Swamiji for advice.

"It would be easy for me to be celibate, but my spouse feels differently. What should I do?"

"Celibacy is a good practice, but if you're married, you can't make that decision on your own." Swamiji then quoted from the Bible, "Thou shalt not *demean* thy spouse."

Sex is one of the strongest human drives. One man, incarcerated for years in a concentration camp, said that even when nearly dead from starvation, many of them still felt sexual longing.

Your wife is dependent on you to fulfill her needs. She can't just switch them off, because you have lost interest. If you abdicate your responsibility, what do you expect her to do?

Sexual frustration in a woman can cause a host of other seemingly unrelated problems, all traceable back to a sense of helpless humiliation and anger rejection brings.

Take this seriously. You are putting your wife in an impossible position. Adultery is not an attractive alternative and I pray she doesn't choose that road. Even without that, you could find your marriage and family falling apart. Whatever you gain from celibacy would be more than offset by the ensuing chaos.

Your wife could turn against the path altogether. That would be unfortunate, not only for the harmony of your home, the welfare of your children, and your ability to peacefully continue with your spiritual practice—it could also jeopardize *her* spiritual future.

The path, to her, would be nothing but a home wrecker. It could take her a long time to get over it.

Sex doesn't have to be about *you*. If you feel no inclination, then let it be an act of selfless love for the mother of your children, the keeper of your home, your companion for life.

Be moderate, uplifted, and attentive to her reality and needs. Let your love making be an offering to Divine Mother, and there will be no spiritual loss, only gain. ❧

*Sex should always
be a gift,
not a responsibility.*

IFT IS A BEAUTIFUL WORD in any context. The problem is that sex, for most people, is not a choice but a compelling need.

If you are in a committed relationship that is not celibate, and you don't feel like offering sex as a gift, you still have a responsibility to care for your partner's needs.

Friendship is the only human relationship entirely free of compulsion. For this reason, Master called it the highest form of love. Nothing binds friends together except the joy they find in one another's company.

A mother's love may be the most selfless. She sacrifices her body to give life to her child. Love and compulsion, though, co-exist. Once conceived, the baby *will* grow within her, and after birth, must be cared for, or it will die.

In the last days of his life, Jesus said to his disciples, "You call me Master, but I call you friend." Krishna, in the Bhagavad Gita, also calls Arjuna "friend." Even between guru and disciple, friendship is the ideal, implying both equality and freedom.

When we think about romantic love in the abstract, the idea of love freely given seems desirable. Many seize upon this as a *principle* of relationships: Love always free, never compelled.

But what is freedom?

The ego defines it as that which is most pleasurable. Applied to romantic love, this means two people stay together as long as it makes them happy. Each freely follows his or her heart, wherever it leads.

Sounds good, until one heart feels the relationship is over, and the other does not. Or it's time for hard truths to be faced and it's easier to run away. When theory collides with reality, hearts get broken.

The error here is that freedom is not of the ego. It's of the soul. No matter how much we indulge the ego's desires, they will never give us the fulfillment we seek. It is not the way we are made.

For a relationship to flourish, the focus has to shift from "What do I *want*?" to "What is my *dharma*?" Dharma is that which leads to expanding awareness.

For a couple to stay together is not always proof of *spiritual* victory. Mere endurance is not the same as expanding consciousness. Dharma is an *inner* definition of right action.

It is more blessed to give than to receive, Jesus said. By *blessed*, he meant *blissful*. As a person matures, he gradually learns that the satisfaction he hoped to find by *indulging* his ego can only be found in *transcending* it.

The ego is the antithesis of freedom. It binds us to the never-ending cycle of likes and dislikes. Transcending the ego is to be even-minded and cheerful in all circumstances.

From the outside, it may look as if a person is bound by obligations. But if those duties are willingly embraced as one's dharma, there is no sense of bondage, only the free will offering of the heart. A gift, as you rightly describe it.

Naturally, not everyone can rise to this level, at least not right away. It takes practice. That's why we are compelled into relationships of all kinds—so that we can practice, over many incarnations, developing the mastery to love selflessly, courageously, and without condition.

In the meantime, we have to be sincere and realistic. "Be practical in your idealism" is how Master put it.

Sex should always be a gift, not a responsibility.

When increased spiritual practice makes sex uninteresting, compared to the bliss one feels in meditation, *that* is the time to leave it behind—unless that means imposing celibacy on a spouse who is otherwise a good partner.

Rather than repudiating responsibility, dharma is to embrace it with calm faith in God. ❧

As newlyweds, moderation in sex is out of the question.

We are deeply dedicated to God; our shared spiritual commitment is the foundation of our relationship. But the sexual magnetism is also strong, and intimacy too satisfying to resist. Should we be concerned?

HE MASTERS SAY sex is one of life's great delusions. Most people consider it one of life's great joys. Not an easy gap to bridge!

Modern society has resolved the dilemma by turning its back on the masters. We swim in a sea of sexual stimulation, and like fish in water, don't even notice. To say women's fashions are immodest is putting it mildly. That which used to be considered pornographic is everyday life in movies, television, and walking down the street.

Little girls are dressed in what would be sexually provocative attire, were they not years from puberty. People think it is cute, not realizing—or caring—that we are teaching a generation of girls to believe feminine beauty is sexual, and ideal love, erotic.

To live even a moderate sexual life these days, what to speak of being celibate, is not easy. In such a restless age, to focus your energy in a committed, loving relationship is a big step forward. When it includes dedication to God, you have the potential for a happy life.

Whether your relationship is pleasing to God is not determined by how often you have sex. Were you not so attracted to each other, you wouldn't be together, and all the other positives would be lost. Overall, your relationship is a big plus.

One of the greatest sources of tension in devotee marriages is sex. One person develops a complex and may decide to renounce sex altogether. Sometimes it is a genuine, spiritually inspired disinclination, but often it is because he or she feels guilty—caught between the desire for God and the desire for sex. The spouse is seen then not as a friend but a *temptation*. And from there, things go rapidly downhill.

I remember a monk who left the monastery to marry. To ease his conscience, he decided he would be celibate. This was not what his wife signed on for. When Swamiji heard about it, he told the man, "You can't have it both ways. If you accept the benefits of a wife, you also have to take the responsibility and consider her reality as well as your own."

Fortunately, the two of you agree. Whatever you do must be an expression of your shared understanding. Doing otherwise will lead to suppression, not transcendence.

Suppression happens when you impose upon yourself external standards of what is "right." Often the imposition is motivated by guilt, or a desire to look good—even if no one but you is looking.

Transcendence happens when you discover *from your own experience* that restraint is more satisfying than indulgence. Discipline may still be needed to manage a desire not wholly disappeared, but it is done with a wholesome attitude. Guilt plays no part in it.

Mahatma Gandhi, famous for his asceticism, summed it up perfectly: "You should never renounce a pleasure until you have replaced it with a higher one."

You transcend sex when your own experience leads you to it. Now, however, is not the time. This is nothing to be ashamed about. It is just where you are.

"Once sex is overcome," Swamiji said, "you can't imagine why you were attracted to it in the first place."

In the meantime, keep in mind some of the ways sex can undercut your spiritual aspirations.

As newlyweds, moderation in sex is out of the question.

Sex is ego-affirming. Ego is the soul identified with the body. Sex not only depends upon that self-definition, it reinforces it.

Sex is compelling. In a refined relationship, sex is based on mutual giving. Still, to the extent that you have personal needs, you cannot be entirely selfless.

Sex emphasizes a unique, personal connection. Most people don't consider this a downside—and it needn't be, if you see your relationship not as an end in itself, but a *starting* point for even greater love. God gives us a special connection with one person to show us our *capacity* for love.

Meditate on these words from the Ananda wedding ceremony: "May our love not be confined by selfish needs, but give us strength ever to expand our hearts until we see all human beings, all creatures as our own. Teach us to love all beings equally in Thee." ∼🥄

My boyfriend thinks "sacred" drugs like LSD are a path to God.

I think the only way to make spiritual progress is to follow the discipline of spiritual practice. What do you think?

SOMETIMES a drug-induced experience is the first step on a person's spiritual journey. It is better (and safer) to awaken without the use of drugs, but in fairness I have to say drugs are sometimes the catalyst.

Repeated drug use, though, is playing Russian roulette with your brain.

The same drugs that induce spiritual experiences can also bring on psychotic states, which don't necessarily go away when the drugs wear off. I've known it to happen even to people who, to that point, had nothing but "spiritual" experiences.

Those who do awaken spiritually through drugs are tapping into their own *samskaras*—latent tendencies from past lives—that sooner or later would have blossomed anyway. If you have spiritual *samskaras,* far better to develop them properly. No saint, master, or true scripture has *ever* suggested finding enlightenment through anything but self-effort.

Richard Alpert (now Ram Dass, author of *Be Here Now*) pioneered the use of LSD in the 1960s. When he went to India the first time, he took his drugs with him. There he met his guru, Neem Karoli Baba. When the subject of drugs came up, the Guru asked to take some. He ingested a double handful of LSD—more pills than anyone had ever thought of taking.

It had no effect.

Ram Dass got the message: Drug-induced states have nothing to do with enlightenment.

"Blessed are the pure in heart, for they shall see God." There is no other way.

Drug experiences, by their very nature, are subjective. The only way to evaluate them is by their long-term effect.

Over the years I have met thousands of devotees, and quite a few habitual users of "sacred" drugs. Many have been likeable, but I have never seen in the drug users the same bright eyes, strength of character, or clarity of mind that I see in those who follow a disciplined spiritual practice.

Drugs train you to think that experiences are there for the taking, rather than as the fruit of *sadhana* (spiritual practices), self-offering, and the grace of God that comes through conscious attunement with a higher vibration.

Spiritual life is about *giving*. Drugs are about *getting*. Look at the fruits of each path and ask yourself, "Who do I want to become?"

When under the influence of drugs, you think you've had a huge change of consciousness, when, in fact, all you've changed is your chemistry. When the drug wears off, you are right back where you started. Or worse.

You have no idea what the drugs might be doing to your brain. Why be the guinea pig in a potentially disastrous experiment?

Before committing your life to this boyfriend, perhaps you should think carefully about whether your core values are compatible. One who defines life by what he can *get* may not be an appropriate partner for one who defines life by what she can *give*. ❧

Isn't wearing distinctive religious garb just spiritual ego?

The whole look of Ananda changed when
the teacher-swamis started dressing in blue.
Why make a distinction between yourselves
and everyone else?

I N THE SUMMER of 2009, Swamiji launched what
he called the *nayaswami order*, a renunciate order for the
New Age. It is a new iteration of the ancient swami order.
Naya means *new*.

The first initiation was a few months later and did, in fact,
change the look of Ananda. In all the years before, people dressed
however they liked. Now everyone in the order wears the color
of the vows they have taken, especially on formal occasions.

Nayaswamis (blue) take a vow of complete renunciation.
The *tyaga* (white) and *brahmacharya* (yellow) vows are for
those who aspire to be nayaswamis, but not yet. Tyaga is for
couples, brahmacharya for single people who intend never to
marry. There is also a *pilgrim* vow (no specific color) for those
raising families, or who want to declare their spiritual intention, but for whom the other vows are not appropriate.

Before this order, Swamiji was the only *sannyasi* among us,
the only one distinctively dressed. Many of us longed to make
an even deeper commitment to God, separating ourselves
more profoundly from the world, and everything it stands for.
For those of us who are married, though, and have vibrant
partnerships, the traditional swami order was not an option,
since joining almost always meant renouncing marriage. A
unique feature of the nayaswami order is that couples can take
initiation together.

The point of special garb is to diminish the ego's hold. It
helps the initiate overcome personal vanity and preoccupation

with outward appearance. It is God-reminding: gold, blue, and white are the colors of the spiritual eye. Blue represents Christ consciousness—a wearable affirmation.

Special clothes also serve to protect against the temptation to dilute one's commitment by wrong or careless action. As the order becomes more established, and the meaning of the garb more widely known, the protective aspect will increase.

Catholic priests and nuns, Buddhist monks, and traditional swamis dressed in their easily recognized habits are treated differently, even by worldly people, out of respect for their vows. Anything that helps maintain the depth of one's commitment is welcome.

It takes courage to declare: "I am not living an ordinary life." Success or failure then is a matter of public record. Far from reveling in the attention this brings, most sincere aspirants shrink from the notoriety. But spiritual cowardice must also be overcome.

When special garb, and the titles that go with it, began to appear at Ananda, a friend who had not taken vows expressed the same concerns you've raised.

"Won't this create divisions and lead to ego?"

"Has anyone who has taken vows put on airs of superiority, or treated you with less kindness and respect than before?" I asked in return. "Have they made you feel excluded from an inner circle to which they now belong?"

"No," she admitted. "In fact, those who have taken vows seem even kinder, and more inclusive."

Theoretically, distinctive dress could foster a sense of superiority. But theory is not the issue; reality is. Look past the colors into the hearts of those wearing them, and I think you will find no cause for concern. ❧

With so many wearing blue, Ananda now looks like a cult.

I'm reluctant to send my friends there. I agree with the ideals behind the nayaswami order, but I prefer a more subtle outward expression. Am I the only one who feels this way?

SWAMIJI FOUNDED the nayaswami order in the late afternoon of June 6, 2009. For several weeks, his health had been declining, and we feared he would not recover. That afternoon he was lying on the couch so still, I thought he might be dead. In fact, in that stillness he was miraculously healed.

He began to speak about founding the nayaswami order, and within fifteen minutes was talking about what the nayaswamis would wear. Special garb is part of formal renunciation. The habit helps define the order.

A few days later, a small group was talking with Swamiji about whether nayaswamis should wear blue all the time. We were talking color and style—long and loose fitting, with a cowl perhaps.

"It would be fine in the rural communities," one man said, "but what about those of us in urban centers. We've spent years trying to fit in!"

Very seriously, Swamiji responded, "Perhaps now is the time to stand out."

Master predicted that hard times are coming. Exactly when, we don't know. But it is obvious that problems are escalating.

The difficulties, Master said, will bring people back to God. Not the Catholic, Jewish, or Islamic God. Not the wrathful, fundamentalist God; but God within: Self-realization, not as a universal reality.

What is needed is more than just "random acts of kindness." The world will not be brought into balance by well-meaning, but nonetheless self-affirming egos, who think they can disregard God and make the world right merely by getting enough other egos to cooperate. They may be sincere, but their methods won't work.

The visible example of people who have given their lives to God in this new way could help inspire others, Swamiji said, especially when times get tough.

To every specific question, though, about what to do, Swamiji replied, "Do as you feel."

The way it has turned out, most nayaswamis rarely walk the streets in robes. Except for formal occasions, the idea of a specific outfit was replaced by "wear what you feel." For most nayaswamis, this means ordinary clothes, but blue. Still, when two or more are gathered together, people notice.

"What's with the blue?"

Four of us were having breakfast in a restaurant. The waitress assumed the blue meant we were Los Angeles Dodgers fans. She was one herself—and wearing blue. We saw no reason to correct her, nodding amiably as she chatted about the recent game.

Swamiji was part of a group of blue-clad nayaswamis going to the Apple computer store. The employees wear the same color—in their case, T-shirts emblazoned with the Apple logo.

An employee, feeling Swamiji's unusual aura, asked us, "Is he the *Archangel of Apple?*"

I wear blue all the time, mostly an oriental-looking tunic and trousers. Strangers tell me how much they love the color. Only when I am with friends wearing similar garments does it occur to them that our clothes may have greater significance. "We've taken a certain initiation," I usually say, or "We're part of a yoga ashram." I would elaborate, but they rarely show interest. Maybe in time they will.

"It's a promise I made to God," I said to some children who asked. We were interrupted before I could say more, so who knows what they took from that!

With so many wearing blue, Ananda now looks like a cult.

The last word on public response was delivered when I was on the road late one night and stopped to get snacks. The only other person in the convenience store was a woman in hip-hop garb. On seeing me, she struck a pose, arms extended, and cried out (loud enough to be heard across the street), "Yo, Mama! You *rock* that blue!"

All these years, we have dressed like everyone else, so people would feel comfortable. The fact is we are different. Our commitment to God and Gurus is nothing like ordinary ego-based living.

Twenty-five years ago, when David and I first arrived in Palo Alto to develop the Ananda colony, just having a guru and practicing meditation put us on the outskirts of society—either the leading edge or the lunatic fringe, depending on your point of view. Since then, society has moved notably closer to what we are doing.

Books about gurus and disciples have spent weeks on the bestseller lists. Meditation classes are offered at the library and YMCA. Yoga has become a major American sport.

Master came to America to lead a spiritual revolution—not walk in a parade. Now that the parade has moved to our side of the street, we need to take the next step—toward where everyone wants to go, but doesn't know how to get there.

Since the order's advent, people who come to Ananda, see us in our temples and on the street, can't help but notice we have made decisions that set us apart.

It is natural to want things to stay the same. Unfortunately, nothing does. Adjusting gracefully—better still, joyfully accepting the inevitable—is one secret to a happy life.

Don't underestimate your friends. Give them a chance to think in new ways. They may surprise you. ❧

Will you be my guru?

I want to set my intention to find God and
am willing to do whatever is needed.

$\mathcal{T}$HE SIMPLE ANSWER is no. The limiting factor is not you; it is I. Some people use the word guru more casually than I do. To me it means a person of Self-realization, a true "dispeller of darkness." I am sincere in my aspirations. I have been on the path many years. Still, it is not appropriate to call myself a guru to you or anyone else.

Our path was founded by avatars and is led by a great disciple. Better to keep our attention focused on the highest source of grace. Otherwise this work will be diluted before one generation has passed.

Having said that, let me balance my *no* with an emphatic *yes* to the real question. "Will I help you in your quest to know God?"

It would be my honor to do so.

I have received from Swamiji so much inspiration and guidance, it is both my privilege and responsibility to pass on to you (and anyone who will listen) as much as I can.

"It is the nature of a happy person to want everyone else in the world to be as happy as he is!" Swamiji said.

This much I *will* claim: this path has made me happy.

Whatever you receive of spiritual benefit through me, is in direct proportion to how much I have gotten myself out of the way. All credit goes to Swamiji, who is the center of my spiritual life, and to the great masters of this line.

You and I are *gurubhais*—sister disciples—walking the path together, trying with all our hearts to be pure instruments of God. In that capacity, I am happy to help, and ask in return that you help me, as all in this spiritual family help one another.. ༺

I may have to kick my adopted son out of the house.

He came to us from a troubled background when he was a child. Now, as a teenager, he is acting in a way that jeopardizes his place in our home. I desperately want to help him, but I can't unless he does his part. How can I give up my attachment to one I love as my own son? Even when I meditate, I don't feel the presence of God sufficiently to compensate for my agonizing sense of loss.

$\mathcal{N}$ONATTACHMENT IS an important principle, but not one a loving mother can easily embrace.

When trying to affirm an attitude you have not yet achieved, it is best to choose one bigger than your present consciousness, but not so large that there is no point of inner connection. If the affirmation is too foreign to your nature, it won't work. In fact, it can actually make things worse.

Every time you focus on that attitude, instead of embracing it, you will pull away. Nonattachment falls into this category for you and is not the right choice.

An acquaintance of mine worked as a chemist. After a number of years, she inexplicably developed allergies to some of the materials she worked with. Overexposure, perhaps. She took a long leave of absence. We spoke just before she was due back at work.

"This is the affirmation I'm using," she said. "*I am healthy and happy. Nothing in this world can take from me my physical, mental, and spiritual perfection.*"

"You don't believe a word of that, do you?"

"*No!*" she replied, with a commitment conspicuously lacking before.

"You need to affirm something you actually believe," I said. "Instead of dissolving your doubts, that affirmation strengthens them. Every time you say it, your subconscious says, '*No!*'"

We came up with this: *Whatever happens, God and I will find a way to go forward in perfect harmony.*

She did have faith in God, and His loving care. She had no faith, however, in her body's ability to be healthy in the presence of those chemicals.

The rule for effective affirmation is: *Go with your strengths.*

She was only an acquaintance, so I don't know what happened when she went back to work. But she left our session happier and more confident than when she walked in.

Life is full of disappointments, at least when viewed from the level of reality on which they occur. Even a dream, Master said, is real on that level.

That is where you are now: in the middle of a dream, about to become a nightmare. You opened your heart to a child needing a home. You committed yourself in a way that cannot be withdrawn merely because what you hoped for him may not happen.

Sister Gyanamata, Master's most advanced woman disciple, wrote many letters to her fellow disciples, published in a book called *God Alone*. It could be a great comfort to you.

She explained that each devotee has to find his or her personal *cornerstone of faith* and build from there. For some, it is the guru. To trust him as an infallible guide is their starting point. For others, it may be the healing power of love, the experience of meditation, the joy of service, the bliss of chanting, the friendship of fellow devotees, or a single revelation so powerful nothing can undermine it.

Whether dramatic or humble, what matters is that it gives you unshakeable faith in the expanded reality revealed.

Nonattachment for you right now is just a word. You need to find your true cornerstone. Difficult experiences force us to go deep within, until we hit the bedrock of faith on which a spiritual life can be built.

I used to struggle with self-doubt. No amount of reassurance from others could resolve my confusion. In an effort to find a way through the chaos, I searched a book of affirmations for one that fit the criteria above—bigger than my present consciousness, but not too big.

I chose this: *I know God's power is limitless, and as I am made in His image, I too have the strength to overcome all obstacles.*

I had faith in the first part: God's power, and my relationship to Him. The last was dicey. I didn't fully believe it; neither could I reject it. It was the inescapable extension of what I already believed.

I said that affirmation for years before it finally beat down my subconscious habit. Not completely, but enough for me to go forward in a new way.

There are few experiences in life more painful than watching someone you love choose a road of inevitable suffering. Master himself wept when certain disciples turned away from the path. Tears streamed down his face—Mother's heart breaking for Her children. Even the Guru, though, could not interfere with their free will.

When I cannot prevent what seems to me preventable disaster, I take refuge in a point of unshakeable belief, also a core principle of Ananda: "Where there is dharma, there is victory." If we do our best to fulfill our dharma, righteousness will ultimately prevail.

The challenge is to live through all that may occur before that righteous end is achieved. I call this "doing your dharma in a vacuum," an empty space where no positive result seems possible.

Sometimes your right action may appear to make the situation worse—like now. If your son refuses to change, he will have to leave. You may feel you are disconnecting yourself from his fate.

Don't think for a moment this is true. The prayers of a loving mother are never lost. God knows your heart, and will store those blessings until your son can receive them. Stick fast to dharma, no matter how sad you may feel.

One time, when people close to me were facing a crisis, I was called upon to help. For their sake, I had to stay calm, but inside I was falling to pieces.

Alone in my car, tears didn't begin to express the pain I felt. A still, small voice interrupted my tears. "Do you think this is happening outside the will of God?"

That's a point of unshakeable faith for me. No matter how tough the karma, I know God is walking us through whatever has to be faced.

I stopped crying, but joy did not replace my despair. Far from it! My heart was broken, and that emotion needed to express.

Master says: "Don't pray as a beggar. Demand of God your divine inheritance!"

The force of my tears now went into a prayer-demand.

"Okay, God. You know what You are doing. But You have to get on with it! Whatever it is You are trying to teach these people, You must help them learn it—and soon!"

When I went back inside, to my astonishment, everything had shifted. The crisis passed. Healing began. Since then, when people suffer, I often talk to God that way. Never again has it worked instantaneously, but it comforts me and helps them.

The man who became St. Augustine was, in his early life, a libertine. His mother was a devout Christian. No matter how far her son wandered from his true path, she never gave up on him. Later, when he awakened to divine realities, he credited his transformation to her prayers.

Replace nonattachment with qualities accessible to a mother's heart: patience, courage, and faith. *Patience* as your son finds his way through life. *Courage* to stand strong in dharma, no matter how your heart may bleed. *Faith* that *where there is right action, there will be victory.* That is God's law, and He *never* breaks His promise. ❧

My elderly mother is bitter and unhappy.

Underneath, I know her heart is kind, but it rarely shows. If she dies with these attitudes, will the angels still be there to greet her?

$\mathcal{G}$OD KNOWS US better than we know ourselves, and is not fooled by the face we show the world. "God reads the heart," as Master put it.

When she dies, your mother will be received into the highest reality she is capable of accepting. Angels will be there to greet her. In the astral world (as in this one), those who are more advanced help those coming up from behind.

There is only so much, however, that those beings can do if your mother is unwilling to give up her wrong understanding. Death alone won't change her.

If her bitterness is just a façade, to protect a tender heart, God will understand. If it is a rejection of divine realities, even God cannot force her to face the Light. Take comfort, it isn't a matter of what she says. It is who she is inside.

Though hard to watch, suffering is a necessary stage on the road to wisdom. It forces us to reflect: "Am I the person I want to be? Is this the life I want to have?"

Introspection opens us eventually to realities formerly rejected. A taste of bliss awakens the desire for more. Gradually we let go of self-imposed bondage to embrace that which brings us closer to the Light.

Perhaps you are now a mother yourself. There are times when a child rebels against what has to be done. Go to school, for example, or learn to share. Or not eat the whole cake in one sitting.

The child may be grief-stricken at what is being imposed. Still, a good mother will not yield. It would not be love but cowardice for her to cave to his emotions when his future is at stake.

So it is with Divine Mother. She knows the future. Only by transcending ego and embracing the Infinite will we find the happiness we seek.

If you want to be a true friend to your mother, you must help her the way Divine Mother does. To pray merely that she be happy is like giving the child the whole cake to stop his crying. You must show the same faith in God you want your mother to have.

Pray that she learn whatever Divine Mother is trying to teach. That she find within herself the courage to move forward.

Your mother has good karma: she raised a devotee who can now pray for her eternal wellbeing.

Be assured, your mother got herself into this, and she can get herself out. Respect her, the way a good mother respects her child. She doesn't panic, merely because the child struggles. She stands by with faith.

Your prayers can be of great benefit, especially if you pray—with faith—that she can and will awaken to higher realities. ❦

My mother has really poor judgment about men.

For twenty years, I've been dealing with the fallout. The most recent husband has (once again) taken all her money, leaving her stone broke, and with a debt higher than I can pay. Even if I could pay it, I am not sure I should. I meditate and practice Kriya, but this whole situation really gets to me. Any suggestions?

W E HAVE THIS sentimental notion that family should be a place of comfort. People are drawn together, however, for a variety of reasons, not all of them positive. Love is magnetic. So is antipathy. Sometimes people come together as a family, Master said, "so they can fight it out at close quarters." Chilling, to be sure, but we see the evidence everywhere.

You have to assume that having a mother like this is karmically appropriate for you. That the challenges she puts in front of you are just what you need to grow spiritually—which is the only goal worth striving for. Your human mother is a gift from your Divine Mother. Resist any thought of being treated unfairly.

This does not mean your mother is behaving well, or that you have to compromise your own life in the name of helping her. You have to act in the best interest of *all* concerned. Sensitivity is needed to discern which choice among many is right for you both.

Obviously, she does not want your advice, or to put it more charitably, is unable to act on whatever advice you may offer. Her karma compels her down this path. Don't waste your time trying to persuade her, if she isn't ready to hear.

It may be appropriate to let the karmic waves crash. Her soul is being guided into hard times so she can learn the consequences of her wrong thinking.

If her problems are bigger than you can handle, accept that it is God's will for you not to solve them. Inwardly, though, much can be done.

My relationship with my parents bears no resemblance to you with yours, but one thing we share: an inability to change someone else.

At the end of their lives, my parents were debilitated; my mother, physically; my father, mentally. It was hard to watch them decline. I had lots of ideas about how to help, but for the most part, they were not interested.

Because of my understanding of life and death, I thought it would be fine to pray that Divine Mother take them out of those aged bodies into astral freedom. This may sound harsh, but death is nothing to fear. When the body becomes untenable, death is a blessing. It seemed to me they had reached that point.

Something about that prayer, though, felt wrong. I realized my main motivation was relieving *my* discomfort. Only secondarily was I thinking about them. It wasn't my place to say they had learned everything life could teach.

Still, I was utterly dismayed. Then it occurred to me: I am not afraid of my own karma. Whatever God sends, I know He will also send the grace to deal with it. Why would it be different for my parents?

Just before he was crucified, Jesus declared: "For this hour was I born."

A stirring comment indeed.

Odd as it may seem, each one of us could make the same declaration, and it would have an identical ring of truth. The present moment is the sum total of all progress so far—and the starting point for all to come.

With my parents, thinking like this relieved some stress, but more was needed. I said, "Thy will be done," but my heart wasn't in it. I began to pray.

My mother has really poor judgment about men.

"Divine Mother, You are in charge; I'm just here to help. These are my parents, but they are Your children. I want for them what I want for myself: spiritual growth. If this is their path to realization, then I accept it gratefully. However, whatever it is they need to learn, You have to give them the devotion, humility, and wisdom to learn it! And please do it now!"

My parents' situation did not notably improve. In fact, as time passed (they lived several more years) things got worse. But no longer did I resist. I didn't run around trying to fix things that weren't broken. Praying this way greatly increased my faith that everything was happening as it should.

Still, I wasn't passive. *And this is important:* All the energy I had put into running around trying to make things different, I now used to hold myself inwardly still. Human emotions surged. Whenever they swept me away, I gathered my strength, came back to center, and made myself receptive again to Divine Mother's will.

I was able to give my parents more selfless love than I ever could have done on my own. I *did* less, but *gave* more. That was my lesson, and everything conspired to help me learn it.

The main thing is, you don't want to see this same karma again. Everything is conspiring to help you learn your lessons, whether to help your mother actively, or to stand aside, and let her karma take its course. Work in partnership with Divine Mother, and She will tell you how best to proceed. ᕧ

Trying to fix
my daughter's hard karma
only makes it worse.

With your parents, you managed to change
your attitude. What was the tipping point?

*I*T STARTED WITH Swamiji's definition of *true maturity* as "the ability to relate to realities other than one's own."

When old age began to manifest with a vengeance in the life of my parents, I wanted to help. But instead of relating to their reality, I thought only of how I would feel in their place. This was neither maturity nor compassion.

I wasn't feeling *them*; I was feeling *me*—like the plot of a movie, where suddenly we had switched places. Naturally such a thing would be disconcerting, and trigger in me exactly what it did: an overwhelming urge to make things different! No calm acceptance. No joy. No belief that God was in charge and doing exactly what He knew was best.

This was not how my parents felt. Sure, old age can be difficult, but for them it wasn't an abrupt switch into another reality. The life they had was the life they had created over eighty years—and incarnations before. It was both inevitable and appropriate, neither an emergency, nor a sudden break from the past. It was simply life as they had always known it, shifted somewhat by time, but still familiar.

That was the first revelation.

The second was even more far-reaching.

I am not afraid of my own karma. I don't walk around worrying about what might happen next. Whatever comes, with the grace of God, I'll get through it, and in the process hopefully become a better person.

I noticed, though, that I did not have the same faith in others. Nor, apparently, did I believe God would help them as I knew He would me. So I tried to resolve their karma for them.

Looking at my parents objectively, I saw they were getting along just fine. Yes, they were struggling, but also bravely facing what had to be faced. I might do things differently, but it wasn't happening to me; it was happening to them.

I took care of my parents to the end of their lives. With this understanding, the help I offered was more closely aligned to their actual needs.

God is in charge. Behave accordingly. 🐦

My son's wife is
a compulsive nail-biter.

I find it unbearable to be in the presence of anyone with a nervous habit like that. Naturally I want to have a relationship with her, but I dread going to visit. I don't know how to handle this.

WHEN I FIND MYSELF in the company of someone who upsets my inner peace—for whatever reason—if I can turn toward God and away from myself,
I can usually change my attitude. Of course, connecting with
God is not easy if one is inwardly disturbed.

A solution came when I was surrounded by a group of beggars in India. I didn't have enough rupees to satisfy them all,
and to give only to some would have made matters worse. Besides, I didn't like their attitude. But they were in need and I
wanted to do something.

Looking calmly into the eyes of those nearest, I prayed,
"Divine Mother, bless us all." The beggars had their reasons to
be agitated. I had mine. We were united by our shared need for
Divine Mother's help. After just a few silent repetitions of this
prayer, a wave of peace descended. The beggars calmed down
and didn't protest when I walked away.

Since then I have used this prayer when confronted by anyone who disturbs my peace or makes demands I can't fulfill.

Nail biting is unpleasant, even in children; one can only
imagine how embarrassing it is for a grown woman, and how
driven she must be to do it. Stand in her shoes. Perhaps compassion will temper your aversion.

What disturbs us about others is always a reflection of what
we find distressing in ourselves. We imagine if we can expunge
these qualities in them, they will also disappear from us. Unfortunately, it doesn't work.

Even if your weaknesses are different from your daughter-in-law's, there has to be a connection. Her nervous habit would not otherwise so mightily disturb your peace.

If it were your son, would your heart be big enough to love him still? If the cause was a brain injury, would you be more accepting? What if it were *you*—injured in a way that caused unpleasant side effects—how would *you* want to be treated? Kindness given to your daughter-in-law now will come back to you through others in your hour of need.

God has sent this woman to help you grow. Sooner or later you will have to expand your heart to include her, and everyone like her—not for their sakes, but for your own peace of mind.

Can you imagine loving someone so much that such a mannerism wouldn't bother you?

Pray for that kind of love. *Divine Mother, bless us all.* ❧

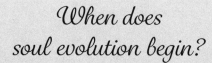

When does
soul evolution begin?

*The masters say we only go through the cycle of
Self-realization once, but doesn't that pit the
linear process of Self-realization against the
non-linear reality of eternity? I don't get it.*

N OR DO I. I can share with you, though, what Master says.

The process of Self-realization is not linear. It is not even a process. We do not *become* anything. We simply *realize* that which has always been true.

Let's say you are walking on a jungle trail and a branch falls across the path. Because of the shape and the way it fell, you think it is a poisonous snake. You draw your weapon, and warn others to stay away. There is nothing pretend about it. You sincerely believe that your life and the lives of others are at risk. But you are wrong.

No matter how committed you are to the delusion—nor how much action, emotion, and self-definition you layer on top—the premise is still false. It never was a snake. It was always a piece of wood.

So it is with the ego. It *appears* to have a separate reality, which we think we have to protect. But no matter how convincing the illusion, the truth is: We are not separate. The only reality is God.

From the ego's perspective, Self-realization takes a long time. Once it comes, however, we see that time itself was part of the illusion. Always, it is the Eternal Now.

Such thoughts cannot be understood from the level of consciousness asking the question. Nor, for that matter, by the one writing the answer.

Master suggested we memorize his poem "Samadhi"—which describes the state of Self-realization—and repeat it in meditation. Through that poem, imbued as it is with Master's cosmic vibration, we glimpse the realm where these truths are not questions and answers, but direct perceptions.

After Swamiji left his body in April 2013, I found repeating "Samadhi" brought him close. Images I had long contemplated took on new life through attunement with his liberated consciousness.

Master tells us that creation is divided into Days and Nights of Brahma. These are unimaginably long cycles of time in which creation is manifested, and then withdrawn into God.

A disciple asked Master, "When a Night of Brahma begins, and creation is withdrawn, do those souls not yet realized have to start all over again?"

"No," Master explained. "Each soul is re-manifested with the new Day of Brahma at the same level it had attained when creation was withdrawn, and continues from that point."

As to when soul evolution begins, from the moment a spring emerges from the earth, each drop of water flows toward the sea. So it is with the soul. All beings seek union with God.

As St. Augustine put it, "Thou hast made us for Thyself, and our hearts are restless until they find their rest in Thee." ❧

If God is Bliss, why did He create suffering?

How much is God involved in the details of our lives? If karma rules everything, what about free will? Did we start free, immediately screw up, and now have to spend the rest of eternity trying to get back to where we were? If so, why did God create us so stupid in the first place?

EVERY TIME IN THESE forty-some years with Swamiji, when I thought he didn't understand a situation, it was always *I* who was at fault. This is not false humility. I am an intelligent person, but it is not about intelligence; it is my level of consciousness.

Fortunately, he was kind enough to explain himself. Invariably, I learned important truths that were outside the realm of my awareness. My understanding of life was like watching a movie. The action starts when the characters appear in the frame, and ends when they disappear from view.

Swamiji was not limited to this narrow perspective. His intuition included karma from past lives, subtle consequences of present decisions, and the interplay of personal and impersonal forces I didn't know were there.

I used to think getting good answers to hard questions was the way to change myself. I have learned that intellectual knowing is not enough. There must also be a change of heart, and a descent of grace.

Do I have free will in any ultimate sense? I know the choices I make in the morning affect the way I feel in the afternoon. The decisions I make this week have consequences next week. And this year is the determining factor in how next year turns out.

Karma is cause and effect, pure and simple.

I can't see into past or future lives, but the evidence I have tells me right action brings right result. Right attitude brings greater happiness. And love conquers all. Further speculation may be interesting, but as Swamiji once said, "What difference would it make?"

I wouldn't live any other way even if I did know. "Sufficient unto the day is the trouble thereof."

Maybe you think if free will is a joke, and your life is pre-determined, you'll take a rain check on personal effort. Stay in bed all day and eat chocolates. Try it. See if it makes you happy.

Maybe my limited sense of free will is only an illusion, but it works for me. I like small questions, because I can do something with the answers. Small changes step-by-step lead to total transformation. This I know from persevering for years, until my own experience revealed the truth.

In answer to why God made the universe, Swamiji said, "It is the nature of Bliss to want to share Itself." If you see a movie you love or find a restaurant with great food, what is the first thing you do? You call a friend and tell him about it. Happiness increases when shared.

So what if your friend goes to the movie and eats at the restaurant, but thinks the movie stupid and the restaurant too noisy? The fact that he didn't enjoy himself does not change *your* experience—nor your joy in telling him about it.

His consciousness drew to him a certain result. Yours drew, from the same circumstances, one entirely different.

So it is with this world. Each one of us experiences it differently. Your perception is revealed in the way you ask the question: "If God is Bliss, why did He create suffering?" Is the world a place of suffering, or is that just how you see it?

Here is why I let the question sit unanswered. Suffering *is* how we see it. Why didn't He make it easier for us to see His Bliss?

I don't know. To understand God you have to experience reality as He does. Your consciousness has to be as large as your question before you can understand the answer. All those who have realized God tell us there is no problem. It is our perception that is at fault.

If you think a friend betrayed you, you may suffer intensely. If it turns out to be a misunderstanding, is your friend still responsible for your suffering?

As for how much God is involved in our lives, answer this question: How much is the ocean involved in the wave? Take any aspect of your life, no matter how minute, and try to define its existence without reference to what has come before. It can't be done.

What limits our free will is not any act of God. We are imprisoned by our own limited consciousness—wrong self-definitions, likes and dislikes that constrict the natural love of the heart.

At first, knowing how we got here and why seems important. We beat on the bars of our cell demanding answers.

"God did it!" someone shouts. "*He* is responsible!"

So we curse God. When that doesn't work, we collapse in despair. Eventually we notice that all this shouting and crying has no effect on our imprisonment. So we ask a different question.

"How do I get out?"

The answer to all cosmic mysteries is this: *Live selflessly. Love God. Serve. Meditate.* Do that and your consciousness will change. Your happiness will increase and you will *experience* the answer. God's ways are not inscrutable when you share in His Bliss.

We blame God for something He never did. It only seemed that way. When God-realization comes, the saints tell us, it is a pure "love fest"—all the sweeter because so long in coming. ✎

Why did God choose
Mary to be the
Mother of Jesus?

*H*ISTORIANS, intellectuals, novelists, politicians, and sociologists have joined theologians now in offering competing theories about Jesus, and what he taught. How can we tell fact from mere speculation? "Look to the saints," Swamiji says. "Only those who have the same state of consciousness as Jesus can speak with authority."

In the last years of his life, Master started rewriting his series of lessons on Self-realization. Unfortunately, he never finished. Swamiji was present when Master dictated the first lesson, which included this astonishing remark: "The wise men who visited Jesus in the manger were three gurus of our path: Babaji, Lahiri Mahashaya, and Sri Yukteswar."

Whether this was an astral visitation, the same souls living a previous incarnation, or the deathless Babaji in his present form, Master did not say. There was, however, some enduring physical reality, because the so-called "lost years of Jesus" were spent in India and Tibet, studying with those same three. Jesus "returned the visit they paid him at birth," Master said. There are many traditions in the East, and ancient documents, confirming this.

The entire life of Jesus was only thirty-three years. Yet all four of the gospels say nothing about him from the ages of twelve to thirty. It is impossible to imagine that when Jesus was with his disciples, the subject of those years never came up, or that his biographers would deliberately omit such a big part of his life.

Avatars—Self-realized masters—incarnate with no karma of their own. They come to show those still striving for Self-realization how to attain it. Discipleship and sadhana are essential. An avatar lives a disciplined life, not from personal need, but to set the example.

Otherwise, his disciples might too easily conclude, "On *your* path you have to meditate and do austerities. But on *ours*, we don't."

A large part of *Autobiography of a Yogi* is about Master's search for his guru, years of training, and continuous effort to realize God. Yet he was *born* Self-realized. He wasn't expressing his own karma. It was a role he had chosen to play.

The same is true for Jesus. At the age of twelve, he went on pilgrimage with his parents to Jerusalem. Then he stayed behind to teach in the temple. When his parents realized he wasn't with the caravan, they rushed back and found him there.

"Why have you done this? See how worried we have been?"

"Why were you looking for me? Do you not know I must be about my Father's business?"

Master said that, soon after this incident, Jesus left home and for the next eighteen years wandered in India, sitting at the feet of great masters and doing sadhana to prepare for the work ahead.

There were no "lost years." His disciples knew, and the account was included in the gospels.

Jesus incarnated during Kali Yuga descending, the darkest age through which our planet passes. Crucifixion, deeply offensive to our present sensibilities, was common practice. Two thieves were crucified next to Jesus, showing how brutal society was at that time.

Kali Yuga reached its nadir in 500 A.D. Soon after, the decision was made to remove from the Bible all reference to those eighteen years.

"People would lose faith if they knew Jesus had to study and make a spiritual effort. What did he have to learn, and who could teach Him? He was the Son of God!"

When Jesus called himself the Son of God, he was not speaking of himself as a person, but the state of realization he had attained: Christ consciousness. His more advanced disciples (including many who came after) understood. But for society as a whole in Kali Yuga, subtle perception was not possible. They defined Jesus by what they could see: his physical body. Church officials did not understand their own master.

"It didn't hurt the faith of Jesus' disciples to hear about his training!" others countered. But their pleas fell on deaf ears, and any reference to those eighteen years was purged.

One proof they were taken out is that those years in the Bible are blank. Church officials had the nerve to remove information, but not invent new facts.

Also removed—at the Second Council of Constantinople, 553 A.D. – were most references to reincarnation. (Some remain. See the chapter "Reincarnation" in *The New Path*.) The logic was similar: "People need to buckle down. If they think they have all the time in the world, they won't make the effort." The pope disagreed and boycotted the council, but counter-arguments were ignored.

How does this relate to Mary?

When the Church removed from Jesus' teachings the necessity for sadhana, the fact of reincarnation, and a true understanding of the guru-disciple relationship, they lost the idea of Self-realization—for everyone but Jesus. And for him, they lost any notion of how he came to be realized.

This is what the Church wanted. With the possibility of individual Self-realization removed (or distorted beyond recognition), the devotee could no longer work for his own salvation. It could only come through Jesus Christ—and the intercession of "His" Church—with blessings, absolutions, and priests as necessary intermediaries between the devotee and God, all substituted for *direct* communion.

Thus Christianity became *Churchianity*. It is not when a religion becomes organized that the damage is done. It is when *the institution makes itself essential to the devotee's salvation.* That is what the Church accomplished.

The other purpose the Church had, besides strengthening its own position, was to elevate Jesus to a unique position he never claimed for himself. Jesus taught Self-realization for all.

"That which I do, ye shall do, and greater things."

"Do not your own scriptures say, 'Ye are gods'?"

"Be ye therefore perfect, even as your Father in heaven is perfect."

These are not compliments; they are *commandments*. Jesus, and all realized masters, are souls *just like us*. What makes them different is that they have achieved perfection. We have a ways to go.

Without reincarnation, one lifetime is not long enough to become "perfect, even as our Father in Heaven is perfect"; so the meaning of that statement, in Churchianity's view, must be other than what it seems. Translations of the Bible have been amended accordingly, offering phrases such as "Be ye therefore good, as your Father in Heaven is good."

Catholic saints who do become Self-realized are an anomaly. There is no context to explain *how* or *why*. The Church persecutes them fiercely—then anoints them after death.

They are persecuted because, without an understanding of Self-realization, saints cast doubt on many key aspects of Churchianity. All priests are ordained equally, for example. What do you do, then, when one, by his holiness, proves himself *more* ordained than the rest?

Bury the evidence as best you can! Those who stand out, the Church confines to their cells, or sends to remote parishes. Padre Pio, for one.

Master said Jesus appeared to Babaji and asked that a divine messenger be sent to the West to restore his original teachings, and show the unity between the undiluted teachings of Jesus and those of Krishna, which have also been compromised.

Master is that messenger. He boldly called his teaching of original Christianity the *Second Coming of Christ*.

"Whenever virtue declines, and vice predominates," the Bhagavad Gita says, "I, the Infinite Lord, take visible form to destroy ignorance and restore righteousness." This is a more accurate view of who these masters are than anything Churchianity offers.

Now to Mary.

Master talked about several of his own previous incarnations, including Arjuna (whose dialogue with his guru, Krishna, is preserved as the Bhagavad Gita), and William the Conqueror. He also identified incarnations of others in our line of gurus. Lahiri Mahasaya was Kabir; also King Janaka. Babaji was Krishna. Sri Yukteswar was William's closest advisor, Lanfranc. Speaking of his disciples, Master said that James J. Lynn (his most advanced male disciple), was one of Arjuna's younger brothers. Daya Mata was William's daughter. Swamiji feels he was William's youngest son, Henry. (*Two Souls: Four Lives* by Catherine Kaivari is a fascinating book about William and Henry.)

In *The New Path* ("His Last Days"), Swamiji explains how families of souls gather around a great master "to work out their salvation—not only inwardly on themselves, but by interaction with one another. To achieve divine emancipation, it is necessary to spiritualize one's relations with the objective world and with other human beings, as well as with God.

"The stronger the family, spiritually speaking," Swamiji continues, "the greater its attractive pull on new souls that may still be wandering in search of an identity of their own. A family evolves with its individual members; at last it, too, becomes a 'star' in the firmament of humanity, and begins to produce great souls of Self-realization.

"As spiritual 'stars,' such great families become powerful for the general upliftment of mankind. . . . Yogananda's is one such spiritual family. His forms part of a greater spiritual 'nation,' of which Jesus Christ and Sri Krishna (in this age, Babaji) are also leaders."

Mary's relationship with Jesus must have been formed many incarnations before. She was one of the "great souls of Self-realization" Swamiji describes, easily able to commune with angels who came, the Bible says, to tell her what was to come.

"Your chosen people have always been those of every race and nation who, with deep love, chose Thee," it says in the Festival of Light.

Then, together, the congregation affirms, "O Lord, with all my heart, with all my mind, with all my soul, and with all my strength, I choose Thy love, I choose only Thee."

Some say Jesus was part of the Essene community, an enlightened group within Judaism that lived by higher teachings than most of their fellow Jews. The Essenes knew an avatar was coming, and the community prepared itself for his birth. They recognized Mary as a special soul, and, according to ancient tradition, trained her from a young age for the role she was to play.

God chose Mary because, long before Jesus was born, with all her heart, mind, soul, and strength, Mary chose God. ❧

Jesus: Son of Man or Son of God?

Is there a difference? I am also confused by the many references to circumcision. Is it allegorical? If so, what does it symbolize?

NONE OF THE THEORIES about the symbolic meaning of circumcision are consistent with the principles of Self-realization. I think the discussion in the New Testament is about the actual practice. To be circumcised was synonymous with being a Jew. It was an outward expression of their covenant with God as the *chosen people*.

Being the chosen people undoubtedly started as a high spiritual principle, but the consciousness behind it was lost by the time of Jesus, and never recovered in Judaism as a whole. I grew up in a Jewish family, and being one of the chosen people was rarely offered as an incentive for greater dedication to spiritual ideals. Mostly it was a cause for pride.

Swamiji corrects this. "Your chosen people have always been those of every race and nation who, with deep love, chose Thee." It pleases me now to have this deeper understanding.

Judaism is a true religion. The foundation prayer, "Hear, O Israel, the Lord our God, the Lord is One," is pure Self-realization. Moses was a great master. He taught *Sanaatan Dharma*, Eternal Truth. By the time Jesus came, however, Judaism as it was practiced, bore little resemblance to the revelations of Moses. It was uncompassionate, legalistic, and ruled by a corrupt priesthood.

Even so, it was still the most elevated religion of the time. And many individuals and groups, like the Essene Community, lived by the highest truths. It was their devotion that attracted an avatar to rejuvenate their faith.

What happened to Judaism in the years between Moses and Jesus is similar to what happened to Christianity from the time of Jesus to Yogananda's coming. Individuals of lesser realization gradually brought the teachings down to something they could comprehend. Sometimes they do it for selfish motive; sometimes they just don't know any better. That is why, time and again, as the Bhagavad Gita explains, avatars come.

Jesus was a rabbi. All his disciples were Jews, as were those who persecuted him. The entire drama took place within the Jewish community. After Jesus died, his followers continued to spread the "Good News," but only among their own people. Instead of embracing this new expression of Judaism, however, most Jews rejected it, first peaceably, then with increasing hostility.

When Paul found all doors into the Jewish community shut in his face, he was too filled with the bliss of Christ's message not to share it. So he preached to the non-Jews. When he began living with the gentiles, he couldn't follow himself, or impose on them, all the rules that defined Judaism. Many of his fellow disciples (all Jews) strongly disapproved, and controversy ensued.

Paul asserted that the salvation Jesus offered was available to "all who received him," as the Gospel of John says. Others said gentiles could be saved, but only if they first became Jews, which meant (among other things) circumcision.

Paul said you could be a "Christian," as he began calling himself, without being a Jew. Feelings ran high, because salvation was literally at stake.

Circumcision is merely physical. And it is only an option for men. It has nothing to do with Self-realization. This is obvious to us, but at the time of these discussions, it wasn't at all.

It was the depths of Kali Yuga, and for most people reality was limited to what the senses could perceive. Masters have the same consciousness, no matter what the age. They can only share their consciousness, though, to the extent society (and individual disciples) can receive it.

From the perspective of Dwapara Yuga, salvation clearly does not depend on circumcision, so we conclude they must have been speaking symbolically. But that imposes Dwapara thinking on Kali Yuga. Insofar as the concept of consciousness was understood at all, it was defined by its physical expression: how you washed your hands, what prayers you said, what you did or refrained from doing. This was the measure of your commitment to God, and the very misunderstanding Jesus came to correct.

"The Sabbath was made for man, not man for the Sabbath," Jesus declared. Rules are not an end in themselves, but a means of achieving right consciousness.

Paul won in the end. Christianity became entirely separate from Judaism, and (ironically) sometimes antagonistic to it. Circumcision lost its "Jews only" character, and the dispute in the Bible became increasingly incomprehensible, especially when Kali Yuga ended and Dwapara began.

Which is why, every so often, a new avatar comes to restore the principles of Sanaatan Dharma. When Master was asked if his message was a new religion, he replied, "It is a new *expression*."

In the Bible, many examples are drawn from everyday life: tending sheep, harvesting wheat, petitioning a king, disciplining servants, stoning an evildoer. To us, these seem exotic and require interpretation. But Jesus was merely using examples to which people could relate.

Nowadays, we don't know what we would do if one of our sheep fell into a ditch on the Sabbath, because—come to think of it—we don't have sheep, nor, for the most part, do we have a Sabbath.

Master talks about airplanes, television, movies, telephones, atomic energy, electricity. Imagine how impossible to grasp those things would be for a contemporary of Jesus. It would be similar to how we feel about wheat, sheep, and kings.

In Dwapara Yuga, a master can talk openly about energy and consciousness. Einstein's revelation that matter *is* energy is universally accepted. In the time of Jesus, the idea that matter was anything but what it appeared to be was, for the masses, absurd.

In this age we are able to relate to cultures across the globe and communicate with them instantly. In Kali Yuga, they didn't know there *was* a globe. Master's mission has been to show the essential unity between the teachings of East and West.

Christianity, as most churches now express it, describes Jesus as a unique phenomenon, the beginning and end of divine revelation—a rather limited view, given the picture of the universe that science now provides. This is why fundamental Christianity is fighting so hard to survive. It is being undermined on all sides by a more expansive view of reality.

A clergyman of my acquaintance actually told me the official position of his church is that the full teachings of Jesus were not present at the time of his crucifixion, but developed over centuries. My friend is also a follower of Self-realization, so I could speak frankly.

"Are you saying Jesus, a Self-realized master, had a limited understanding of his own teachings? That he needed the help of theologians coming after to develop them?"

My friend laughed. He had the humility to acknowledge the self-serving logic under which he had been trained.

Now to the Son of Man vs. the Son of God.

Most of Jesus' teachings in the Bible are taken from his public talks. Because it was Kali Yuga, he had to speak through parables that only "those who had ears to hear" could understand.

Master could talk about God beyond and within creation, but Jesus had to speak of the Father and the Son. Few would have understood more explicit explanations of consciousness. The subtle teachings, Jesus gave to his disciples in private.

Jesus, like all avatars, incarnated as a human being. He had parents, a physical body, and a childhood like everyone else. Yes, Jesus was able to resurrect his body, but that was part of the distinction between the Son of Man and the Son of God.

The Son of Man was physical, subject to material laws; the Son of God was not. After Jesus died, and Christianity began to transform itself into what we now have, people felt the need to emphasize his unique nature. This gave rise to dogmas like the Immaculate Conception and the Virgin Birth.

Master skirted these issues, addressing them rarely, and even then with a light touch. "It was not the time," Swamiji explained. "The controversy would have detracted from his real message." Master did call his work the Second Coming of Christ, but he never brought that idea to as fine a focus as he might have, for the same reason. When Swamiji asked, "Were you Jesus?" Master replied, "What difference would it make?"

Much of the confusion people have in reading the Bible, and the chaos caused by sectarian interpretations, comes from the word "*I*." Who or What was Jesus referring to when he spoke of himself as "I"?

Fundamentalists say he was speaking of the unique incarnation called Jesus. They declare that Jesus was the Son of God—but are fuzzy as to how that one physical body could be the *only* Son of God for all time. Since they believe that Jesus is unique, however, they can just say so, and leave it at that.

Self-realizationists reading the Bible know that there have been many avatars, all expressing the same infinite consciousness. The fact that others are equal does not diminish Jesus. An avatar lives within a physical body, but that body does not define him.

The "I" defining an avatar is the Christ consciousness—the divine spirit within him, and within all of us. "I and my Father are One."

Jesus emphasized a point that has been lost in modern Christianity: *All of us* must rise to his state of realization. "To all those who received Him, to them gave he the power to become the Sons of God."

Jesus did live in a physical body, as a man among men, and when he wanted to emphasize that aspect of his mission, he called himself the *Son of Man*. When he wanted to speak of himself as the infinite consciousness, which expressed through that body but *was not defined by it*, he called himself the *Son of God*.

As the Son of God, he declared himself to be one with God. For that he was crucified. For no man, according to the orthodox tradition of the time, can be God. Jesus never claimed that the Son of *Man* was God. To see God, we must transcend all physical limitation, which Jesus proved by his resurrection..

"That which I do, ye shall do, and greater things."

Remember that.

Translators have often used these terms incorrectly. Apply this understanding, though, and you will see that Jesus makes perfect sense. ﹋

(And now, for a complete change of pace!)

I feel so guilty that my Great Dane was put to sleep.

We lost our house in the downturn, and I had to find a home for her. It didn't work out, and her new owners blame me. Losing our house and giving away my dog was sad and stressful, but I never questioned God. Now I can't get over my guilt and grief.

*Y*OU WERE FORTUNATE to have had such a close relationship with your pet. And she was fortunate to have spent so much of her life with you.

The life span of most animals is shorter than that of the humans caring for them, so loving a pet often means living through its death. The life and death decisions we make for our pets are complex and important to many, so I am going to write about it at length.

I have never experienced the kind of bond with an animal that you had, but I have seen it between my husband and his cat. Part of the "dowry" David brought to our marriage was a black female cat named Huey. He had adopted her when she was small enough to fit in his cupped hands, and fifteen years later they had been through a lot: living in different cities, starting several successful enterprises, coming to Ananda.

To say Huey was a disciple would be an overstatement. No matter how sentimentally we might regard her spiritual advancement, she was, after all, just a cat. She was the only cat, however, allowed into Crystal Hermitage, where Swamiji had his home. We lived next door, and when he gave satsang, Huey often came.

I didn't grow up with pets, but I cultivated Huey as a friend. Her relationship with David predated mine. I didn't want to put him in the awkward position of having to choose between us.

I came home one day to find David and Huey sharing quality time. Like any cat, Huey was acutely aware of her surroundings, and registered my arrival with slight tension. "Don't worry," David whispered, petting her gently, "she's one of us."

Two years after we married, we were on a lecture tour and, not for the first time, left Huey with friends. We were in Houston when the call came. "Huey has disappeared." She was always regular in her habits, even when David was away. "It's been three days since she came home. We've searched every crevice, and called for her everywhere. She's gone."

Huey was seventeen. Either she went away to die by herself, as cats often do, or was eaten by something larger. I believe she stayed around long enough to be sure I wasn't going anywhere. Knowing David would be cared for, she felt free to leave.

No matter how close our bond, animals—like all living creatures—have their own destiny. We no more own our pets than we do our children.

Swamiji remarked that he saw *all* beings as just "egos on a spectrum between bondage and freedom, striving to be free." We manifest the body that allows us to express our full potential at that time.

Animals sometimes show an amazing capacity for loyalty, love, and self-sacrifice. Still, they lack the self-awareness needed to make conscious, spiritual progress. That is what distinguishes them from us—no matter how advanced the animal, or how primitive the human.

An animal has an individual ego, or (perhaps more accurately) the full potential of what will become its individual ego when it advances up the spectrum of consciousness. They progress more or less automatically through lower stages of development until their consciousness reaches the point where no animal body can sufficiently express it.

Master says dogs, horses, and monkeys are the most advanced. (Sorry, all you cat lovers, but that's what he says.)

I feel so guilty that my Great Dane was put to sleep.

Once we reach the human level, going back to being an animal is rare, and even if, as punishment for egregious behavior, or in longing for a less conscious life, we do go back, it is usually for only one lifetime.

When we reach the limit of each body's ability to serve our consciousness, we shed it with no more consequence than taking off a jacket when the weather turns warm. Animals relate to their bodies impersonally. Humans get attached to the body they inhabit and generally view its impending loss with more concern than is warranted.

It is good karma for an animal to live with humans. For animals, too, environment is stronger than will power. Being in human company helps speed a pet's evolution.

Animals don't have sufficient awareness to reflect on their condition. They can't speculate, for example, about how their species is treated in emerging economies, where dogs often live on the streets by wit alone—as opposed to the life of ease the average American canine enjoys.

I recall how amused a visiting friend from India was by our dog-grooming salons. The towels were thicker than those in most Indian hotels!

Animals experience both positive and negative emotions. But a great deal of suffering is caused by the thought that things ought to be different than they are. This requires an ability to compare one situation to another. No doubt your Great Dane was highly intelligent, but she simply didn't have the awareness to contemplate, for example, the contrast between her life and that of her littermates.

As a result, animals are more accepting of their destiny. Even the loss of their bodies doesn't grieve them the way we imagine. We should be compassionate, and do our best to alleviate suffering, but also careful, lest attachment lead to decisions not in the best interest of the animals we love.

Huey was most likely eaten. There had been no sign of sickness, or even old age. We lived in the woods. Animals got eaten all the time.

She wasn't much of a hunter. Occasionally, she brought David the gift of a mouse or bird she had killed herself. She showed no remorse. In fact, she seemed proud of what she had done. It was her nature to hunt.

A larger creature sustains itself on the flesh of those weaker. We think it horrific, but for animals who kill to eat, and even for those eaten, it is the appropriate expression of their level of consciousness. When the animal grows beyond that, it no longer incarnates as hunter or prey.

Humans weep over Nature's cruelty. But if we rebel against what is, and choose to grieve about such a fundamental aspect of creation, there will be no end to our sorrow.

Master saw it impersonally. He said to Swamiji once, "God eats people," illustrating his point with a gobbling sound as he lifted imaginary people to his mouth. Almost no one on the planet now will be here a hundred years hence.

Do you think your dog wanted to be a Great Dane forever? It was nice while it lasted, but really, when you think about it, how much fun could it be? Would you condemn her to a dog's life one moment longer than would benefit her spiritually?

Autobiography of a Yogi is one of the most influential books of our time. Almost everyone who veers from traditional religion looking for a more personal spiritual path reads it. It is, for many, their introduction to the whole concept of Self-realization.

Master understood the book's importance, and carefully considered what to include. That he chose to write so movingly about his own pet fawn has always intrigued me.

"We had many pets," Master said of his boys' school in Ranchi, "including a young deer, who was fairly idolized by the children. I too loved the fawn so much that I allowed it to sleep in my room."

He goes on to tell of the deer's death. Master went away for the day, and the deer (despite strict instructions) was fed an excessive amount of milk and collapsed from overfeeding.

Master prayed mightily that the animal be spared. The deer was starting to recover, when its spirit came to Master in a dream.

"You are holding me back," the deer implored. "Please, let me go!"

Master's love was actually hindering its progress. Realizing his mistake, he released the deer. It died shortly after.

Master included this story, I believe, because so many people need to understand how to relate to animals in a greater context.

Early in my Ananda life, I often counseled people, but lacked the maturity at times to speak appropriately. Once, someone complained to Swamiji about something I had said.

I knew I had spoken the truth and Swamiji agreed. But as he explained, even truth should be offered only when a person is ready for it. Otherwise, the person will both reject the advice and be less open to hearing it later.

I felt terrible. I had been trying to be helpful, but had seemingly caused more harm than good. I offered to resign as a counselor, but Swamiji wouldn't let me.

"We are responsible for our *intentions*," he said. "We can't always predict, and we certainly cannot control, how our good intentions will be received."

Then he added, "God reads the heart. He alone never misunderstands. That's what matters most."

It was a great comfort to me then, and has been a guiding principle for me ever since.

You did the best you could. You were careful to find your pet a good home. That it did not turn out the way you intended is not a sign of failure, nor is it anything to feel guilty about.

We give ourselves too much credit and too much blame. We think our little decisions determine the course of destiny. In fact, we are always acting as part of a greater whole. We are instruments, merely, not the source of what happens.

"Parents create the physical body of their child as the vehicle through which a soul can express its destiny," Swamiji said. "Parents do not, however, create either the soul or its destiny."

The spark of divinity you knew as your Great Dane was neither created nor destroyed by you. You merely lived for a time side by side.

Your dog needed to have one more experience before she was done. Merely because the experience was unpleasant (or so you imagine) does not mean it wasn't an important one for her to have.

Had you been the one to put her to sleep, I suspect you would have felt even worse. Perhaps your dog wanted to spare you, so she arranged to be far away. That is as likely as the explanation you've chosen, that you alone are responsible.

God, in other words, has a plan. When we see it unfolding, we have to accept with gratitude whatever He brings.

Swamiji defined humility as self-honesty. This is a brilliantly clear, and subtle, definition. Self-honesty means seeing things as they are.

Let's say you are the best violinist on the planet. The ego might cling proudly to that as evidence of its own worth. But consider how many inhabited planets there may be in this one galaxy alone. Are you the best in the galaxy?

A century from now will you still be remembered? Even were your praises sung for *three* centuries, compare being a violinist to being a Self-realized master directing the destiny of ages.

I feel so guilty that my Great Dane was put to sleep.

Developing any talent to perfection is, at the same time, a notable *spiritual* achievement. The concentration, discipline, and willpower needed to play the violin will serve you well when your aspirations expand to Infinity.

Humility is to see things as they are.

Guilt, by contrast, creates a distorted view. You meant well. You did your best. But your dog had a destiny of her own that was always out of your hands. Think of that fawn, appearing to Master in the dream, pleading for freedom.

Leave room in your thinking for God, and His plans.

Then follow His ways in this, as we do in all things. ∞

Other books by the same author

**SWAMI KRIYANANDA
AS WE HAVE KNOWN HIM**

LOVED AND PROTECTED
**Stories of Miracles and
Answered Prayers**

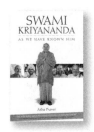

SWAMI KRIYANANDA
AS WE HAVE KNOWN HIM

Asha Praver

The greatness of a spiritual teacher is only partially revealed by the work of his own hands. The rest of the story is one he cannot tell for himself. It is the influence of his consciousness on those who come in contact with him—whether for a brief moment, or for a lifetime of spiritual training. This is the story told here.

Swami Kriyananda, a foremost disciple of Paramhansa Yogananda (author of *Autobiography of a Yogi*) was prodigiously creative in his service to his Guru. His books are available in 28 languages in 100 countries. His music is performed around the world. In India, millions of people watch his daily television show. He founded schools and retreats, and communities on three continents. He spoke eight languages, and circled the globe dozens of times lecturing and teaching.

In this "biography of consciousness," Swami Kriyananda's remarkable qualities are revealed with breathtaking clarity—love for God, divinely guided strength, joy in the face of adversity, humor, wisdom, compassion, and unconditional love. Here, in some two hundred stories spanning more than forty years, personal reminiscences and private moments with this beloved teacher become universal life lessons for us all.

The original 1946 unedited edition of Yogananda's spiritual masterpiece

AUTOBIOGRAPHY OF A YOGI
Paramhansa Yogananda

Autobiography of a Yogi is one of the best-selling Eastern philosophy titles of all time, with millions of copies sold, named one of the best and most influential books of the twentieth century. This highly prized reprinting of the original 1946 edition is the only one available free from textual changes made after Yogananda's death. Yogananda was the first yoga master of India whose mission was to live and teach in the West.

In this updated edition are bonus materials, including a last chapter that Yogananda wrote in 1951, without posthumous changes. This new edition also includes the eulogy that Yogananda wrote for Gandhi, and a new foreword and afterword by Swami Kriyananda.

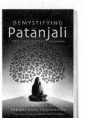

DEMYSTIFYING PATANJALI
The Yoga Sutras (Aphorisms)
The Wisdom of Paramhansa Yogananda
by Swami Kriyananda

What happens as we grow spiritually? Is there a step-by-step process that everyone goes through—all spiritual seekers—as they gradually work their way upward, until they achieve the highest state of Self-realization? About 2200 years ago, a great spiritual master of India named Patanjali presented humanity with a clear-cut, step-by-step outline of how all truth seekers and saints achieve divine union. He called this universal inner experience and process "yoga" or "union." His collection of profound aphorisms—a true world scripture—has been dubbed Patanjali's Yoga Sutras.

Now, a modern yoga master—Paramhansa Yogananda—has resurrected Patanjali's original revelations. Swami Kriyananda shares Yogananda's crystal clear and easy-to-grasp explanations of Patanjali's aphorisms.

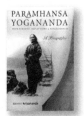

PARAMHANSA YOGANANDA

A Biography with Personal Reflections
and Reminiscences *by Swami Kriyananda*

Yogananda's classic *Autobiography of a Yogi* is more about
the saints Yogananda met than about himself—in spite
of Yogananda's astonishing accomplishments.

Now, one of Yogananda's direct disciples relates the untold story of this
great spiritual master and world teacher: his teenage miracles, his challenges in coming to America, his national lecture campaigns, his struggles to fulfill his world-changing mission amid incomprehension and
painful betrayals, and his ultimate triumphant achievement. Kriyananda's subtle grasp of his guru's inner nature reveals Yogananda's many-
sided greatness. Includes many never-before-published anecdotes.

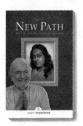

THE NEW PATH

My Life with Paramhansa Yogananda
Swami Kriyananda

WINNER

2010 Eric Hoffer Award for Best Self-Help/Spiritual Book
2010 USA Book News Award for Best Spiritual Book

This is the moving story of Kriyananda's years with Paramhansa Yogananda, India's emissary to the West and the first yoga master to spend
the greater part of his life in America. When Swami Kriyananda discovered *Autobiography of a Yogi* in 1948, he was totally new to Eastern
teachings. This is a great advantage to the Western reader, since Kriyananda walks us along the yogic path as he discovers it from the moment of his initiation as a disciple of Yogananda. With winning hon-
esty, humor, and deep insight, he shares his exciting journey along the
spiritual path.

Through more than four hundred stories of life with Yogananda,
we tune in more deeply to this great master and to the teachings he
brought to the West. This book is an ideal complement to *Autobiography of a Yogi*.

THE ESSENCE OF THE BHAGAVAD GITA

Explained by Paramhansa Yogananda
As Remembered by his disciple,
Swami Kriyananda

Rarely in a lifetime does a new spiritual classic appear that has the power to change people's lives and transform future generations. This is such a book.

This revelation of India's best-loved scripture approaches it from a fresh perspective, showing its deep allegorical meaning and its down-to-earth practicality. The themes presented are universal: how to achieve victory in life in union with the divine; how to prepare for life's "final exam," death, and what happens afterward; and how to triumph over all pain and suffering.

"It is doubtful that there has been a more important spiritual writing in the last fifty years .... What a gift! What a treasure!" —**Neale Donald Walsch**, author of *Conversations with God*

REVELATIONS OF CHRIST

Proclaimed by Paramhansa Yogananda
Presented by his disciple, Swami Kriyananda

The rising tide of alternative beliefs proves that now, more than ever, people are yearning for a clear-minded and uplifting understanding of the life and teachings of Jesus Christ.

This galvanizing book, presenting the teachings of Christ from the experience and perspective of Paramhansa Yogananda, one of the greatest spiritual masters of the twentieth century, finally offers the fresh perspective on Christ's teachings for which the world has been waiting. This work gives us an opportunity to understand and apply the scriptures in a more reliable way than any other: by studying under those saints who have communed directly, in deep ecstasy, with Christ and God.

"Kriyananda's revelatory book gives us the enlightened, timeless wisdom of Jesus the Christ in a way that addresses the challenges of twenty-first-century living."

—**Michael Beckwith**, Founder and Spiritual Director, Agape International Spiritual Center, author of *Inspirations of the Heart*

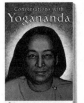

CONVERSATIONS WITH YOGANANDA

Recorded, Compiled, and Edited with commentary by his disciple, Swami Kriyananda

Here is an unparalleled, firsthand account of the teachings of Paramhansa Yogananda. Featuring nearly 500 never-before-released stories, sayings, and insights, this is an extensive, yet eminently accessible treasure trove of wisdom from one of the 20th century's most famous yoga masters. Compiled and edited with commentary by Swami Kriyananda, one of Yogananda's closest direct disciples.

THE ESSENCE OF SELF-REALIZATION

The Wisdom of Paramhansa Yogananda
Recorded, Compiled, and Edited by his disciple, Swami Kriyananda

With nearly three hundred sayings rich with spiritual wisdom, this book is the fruit of a labor of love. A glance at the table of contents will convince the reader of the vast scope of this work. It offers as complete an explanation of life's true purpose, and of the way to achieve that purpose, as may be found anywhere.

WHISPERS FROM ETERNITY

Paramhansa Yogananda
Edited by his disciple, Swami Kriyananda

Many poetic works can inspire, but few, like this one, have the power to change your life. Yogananda was not only a spiritual master, but a master poet, whose verses revealed the hidden divine presence behind even everyday things. This book has the power to rapidly accelerate your spiritual growth, and provides hundreds of delightful ways for you to begin your own conversation with God.

"This is one of my all-time favorite books."—**Krysta Gibson**, *New Spirit Journal*

THE WISDOM *of* YOGANANDA SERIES

This series features writings of Paramhansa Yogananda not available elsewhere—including many from his earliest years in America—in an approachable, easy-to-read format. The words of the Master are presented with minimal editing, to capture his expansive and compassionate wisdom, his sense of fun, and his practical guidance.

HOW TO BE HAPPY ALL THE TIME

The Wisdom of Yogananda Series, VOLUME 1

Yogananda powerfully explains virtually everything needed to lead a happier, more fulfilling life. Topics include: looking for happiness in the right places; choosing to be happy; tools and techniques for achieving happiness; sharing happiness with others; balancing success and happiness; and many more.

KARMA AND REINCARNATION

The Wisdom of Yogananda Series, VOLUME 2

Yogananda reveals the truth behind karma, death, reincarnation, and the afterlife. With clarity and simplicity, he makes the mysterious understandable. Topics include: why we see a world of suffering and inequality; how to handle the challenges in our lives; what happens at death, and after death; and the purpose of reincarnation.

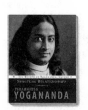

SPIRITUAL RELATIONSHIPS

The Wisdom of Yogananda Series, VOLUME 3

This book contains practical guidance and fresh insight on relationships of all types, including: how to cure bad habits that can end true friendship; how to choose the right partner; how to conceive a spiritual child; and the Universal Love behind all relationships.

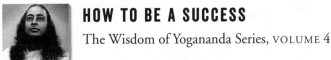

HOW TO BE A SUCCESS

The Wisdom of Yogananda Series, VOLUME 4

Expand your search for success by knowing how to attract it. By focusing on our *inner* attitudes, Yogananda shows us how to attract what we want in life. This fascinating edition includes the complete text of *The Attributes of Success*, the original booklet later published as *The Law of Success*. In addition, you will learn how to find your purpose in life, develop habits of success and eradicate habits of failure, develop your will power and magnetism, and thrive in the right job.

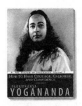

HOW TO HAVE COURAGE, CALMNESS, AND CONFIDENCE

The Wisdom of Yogananda Series, VOLUME 5

WINNER *2010 International Book Award: Best Self-Help Title*

Thousands are learning how to transform their lives with this powerful book. How to dislodge negative thoughts and depression. Uproot fear and thoughts of failure. Cure nervousness and eliminate worry from your life. Overcome anger, sorrow, oversensitivity, and a host of other troublesome emotional responses that can hold us back from our own natural confidence.

HOW TO ACHIEVE GLOWING HEALTH AND VITALITY

The Wisdom of Yogananda Series, VOLUME 6

Paramhansa Yogananda offers practical, wide-ranging, and fascinating suggestions on how to have more energy and live a radiantly healthy life. The principles in this book promote physical health and all-round well-being, mental clarity, and ease and inspiration in your spiritual life.

Readers will discover the priceless Energization Exercises for rejuvenating the body and mind, the fine art of conscious relaxation, and helpful diet tips for health and beauty.

SELF-EXPANSION THROUGH MARRIAGE

A Way to Inner Happiness
Swami Kriyananda

Marriage, understood and lived expansively, is a path to transcendent love—to realization of one's higher spiritual potential. This practical and inspiring guide will help you follow the deeper call of your relationship, enriching not only your marriage, but your life.

MEDITATION FOR STARTERS

Swami Kriyananda

Have you wanted to learn to meditate, but just never got around to it? Or tried "sitting in the silence" only to find yourself too restless to stay more than a few moments? If so, *Meditation for Starters* is just what you've been looking for—and with a companion CD, it provides everything you need to begin a meditation practice.

Filled with easy-to-follow instructions, beautiful guided visualizations, and answers to important questions on meditation, the book includes: what meditation is (and isn't); how to relax your body and prepare yourself for going within; and techniques for interiorizing and focusing the mind. The benefits of meditation are innumerable!

AWAKEN TO SUPERCONSCIOUSNESS

Swami Kriyananda

This popular guide includes everything you need to know about the philosophy and practice of meditation, and how to apply the meditative mind to resolve common daily conflicts in uncommon, superconscious ways.

Superconsciousness is the hidden mechanism at work behind intuition, spiritual and physical healing, successful problem solving, and finding deep and lasting joy.

LIVING WISELY, LIVING WELL

Swami Kriyananda

WINNER *2011 International Book Award:*
Best Self-Help Motivational Title

Want to transform your life? Get inspired, uplifted, and motivated? Here are 366 practical ways to improve your life—a thought for each day of the year. Each reading is warm with wisdom, alive with positive expectation, and provides simple actions and thought-provoking ideas that will bring a new-found sense of joy to your life.

THE RUBAIYAT OF OMAR KHAYYAM EXPLAINED

Paramhansa Yogananda, edited by Swami Kriyananda

The *Rubaiyat* is loved by Westerners as a hymn of praise to sensual delights. In the East its quatrains are considered a deep allegory of the soul's romance with God, based solely on the author Omar Khayyam's reputation as a sage and mystic. But for centuries the meaning of this famous poem has remained a mystery. Now Paramhansa Yogananda reveals the secret import and the "golden spiritual treasures" hidden behind the *Rubaiyat*'s verses—and presents a new scripture to the world.

EDUCATION FOR LIFE

Swami Kriyananda

A brilliant alternative to what has been called the disaster of modern education; the statistics of illiteracy, drug abuse, and violence speak for themselves. In this book, Kriyananda traces the problems to an emphasis on technological competence at the expense of spiritual values, which alone can give higher meaning to life. *Education for Life* offers parents, educators, and concerned citizens everywhere techniques that are both compassionate and practical.

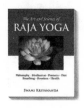

THE ART AND SCIENCE OF RAJA YOGA
Swami Kriyananda

This book contains fourteen lessons in which the original yoga science emerges in all its glory—a proven system for realizing one's spiritual destiny. This is the most comprehensive course available on yoga and meditation today. Over 450 pages of text and photos give you a complete and detailed presentation of yoga postures, yoga philosophy, affirmations, meditation instruction, and breathing practices. Also included are suggestions for daily yoga routines, information on proper diet, recipes, and alternative healing techniques.

THE ART OF SUPPORTIVE LEADERSHIP
A Practical Guide for People
in Positions of Responsibility
J. Donald Walters (Swami Kriyananda)

You can learn to be a more effective leader by viewing leadership in terms of shared accomplishments rather than personal advancement. Drawn from timeless Eastern wisdom, this book is clear, concise, and practical—designed to produce results quickly and simply. Used in training seminars in the U.S., Europe, and India, this book helps increase effectiveness, creativity, and team building in companies everywhere.

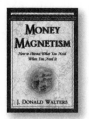

MONEY MAGNETISM
How to Attract What You Need When You Need It
J. Donald Walters (Swami Kriyananda)

This book can change your life by transforming how you think and feel about money. According to the author, anyone can attract wealth: "There need be no limits to the flow of your abundance." With true stories and examples, Swami Kriyananda vividly—sometimes humorously—shows you how the principles of money magnetism work, and how you can start applying them today to achieve greater success in your material and your spiritual life.

LOVED AND PROTECTED

Stories of Miracles and Answered Prayers
Asha Praver

If we ask God for help, will He respond? The stories in this book answer loud and clear: "YES!"

In extraordinary accounts, we see the Divine Hand moving people out of harm's way, healing life-threatening injuries and diseases, providing important guidance for life-and-death, split-second decisions, illuminating hearts and spirits darkened by fear or despair . . . and so much more

A book for those who want a deeper, more trusting relationship with God, and find inspiration in the stories of others who seek also to know Him.

HOW TO MEDITATE

A Step-by-Step Guide to the Art & Science of Meditation
Jyotish Novak

This clear and concise guidebook contains everything you need to start your practice. With easy-to-follow instructions, meditation teacher Jyotish Novak demystifies meditation—presenting the essential techniques so that you can quickly grasp them. Since it was first published in 1989, *How to Meditate* has helped thousands to establish a regular meditation routine. This newly revised edition includes a bonus chapter on scientific studies showing the benefits of meditation, plus all-new photographs and illustrations.

THE TIME TUNNEL

A Tale for All Ages and for the Child in You
Swami Kriyananda

This story explores life-enhancing spiritual truths through the eyes of two young boys, including how to find true happiness, what qualities bring unhappiness, how positive expectations bring positive results, and what values are important. Richly imaginative and inventive, *The Time Tunnel* conveys deep truths in a way that will provide adults and children with fascinating topics for discussion.

CRYSTAL CLARITY PUBLISHERS

Crystal Clarity Publishers offers additional resources to assist you in your spiritual journey. Please visit our website to view all our available titles in books, as well as other products—audiobooks, spoken word, music, and DVDs.

Crystal Clarity Publishers / www.crystalclarity.com
14618 Tyler Foote Rd. / Nevada City, CA 95959
TOLL FREE: 800.424.1055 or 530.478.7600 / FAX: 530.478.7610
EMAIL: clarity@crystalclarity.com

ANANDA WORLDWIDE

Ananda Sangha, a worldwide organization founded by Swami Kriyananda, offers spiritual support and resources based on the teachings of Paramhansa Yogananda. There are Ananda spiritual communities in Nevada City, Sacramento, Palo Alto, and Los Angeles, California; Seattle, Washington; Portland and Laurelwood, Oregon; as well as a retreat center and European community in Assisi, Italy, and communities near New Delhi and Pune, India. Ananda supports more than 140 meditation groups worldwide.

For more information about Ananda Sangha, communities, or meditation groups near you, please call 530.478.7560 or visit www.ananda.org.

THE EXPANDING LIGHT

Ananda's guest retreat, The Expanding Light, offers a varied, year-round schedule of classes and workshops on yoga, meditation, and spiritual practice. You may also come for a relaxed personal renewal, participating in ongoing activities as much or as little as you wish. The beautiful serene mountain setting, supportive staff, and delicious vegetarian food provide an ideal environment for a truly meaningful, spiritual vacation.

For more information, please call 800.346.5350 or visit www.expandinglight.org.